**BBC RADIO**

# T⚬DAY

## PROGRAMME

# PUZZLE
# BOOK 2

BBC RADIO 4

# TODAY
## PROGRAMME

# PUZZLE BOOK 2

## Over 250 brainteasers from the land, sea and ice

Puzzles from 'The Lost Meteorites of Antarctica' team, the Royal Institution, the Royal Academy of Engineering, Puzzle Olympiads and many more

With a foreword by Sarah Sands and introductions by Tom Feilden

CASSELL ILLUSTRATED

# CONTENTS

# FOREWORD

The second *Today Programme Puzzle Book* confirms what we suspected when we published our first book. The country is blessed with quick-witted coders, mathematicians and puzzle solvers who are as sharp as pins at 6:47am. That is the moment when our *Today* presenters take a breath and challenge the nation to a riddle or a disguised sum. I have heard from CEOs who solve it while shaving, others who have to write it down. Parents and children sometimes solve it together before school.

The difference between Book 1 and Book 2 is that we now have far more teachers, students and university lecturers involved in compiling our puzzles. The *Today* programme broadcasts regularly from universities, and a highlight is for a professor or student to read out the puzzle they have created. The live audience is up for trying, even though the spirit can sometimes be more willing than the mind. We hear spontaneous applause and laughter for the puzzle master. Teachers, too, have come out of the classroom to devise puzzles for us, making them school celebrities. Our maths wizard Bobby Seagull is an indefatigable puzzle maker, delighting audiences with his scenarios, often involving football fixtures.

The *Today* programme puzzle has become an institution, as much a part of the programme as the time checks. Where we go, the puzzle goes. So this year we have particularly enjoyed our puzzles from the Arctic, compiled by the top scientists who are working on tackling climate change. What could be a better reminder of global priorities than a puzzle about polar bears?

Sarah Sands, editor of the *Today* programme

# INTRODUCTION

Year two, and I think the #PuzzleForToday is really getting into its stride – a quirky mix of intelligence, inquiry, wit and humour. Who knew you could find inspiration for a puzzle in the Notting Hill Carnival, leaves on the line, hip replacements or the kitchen sink drama that is doing the washing up?

Getting out on the road has helped. Regular listeners will know that the *Today* programme is taking its mission to get to the heart of the news, wherever it's happening, more literally than ever before. That's meant outside broadcasts from Syria to Sweden, Gaza, Tripoli and Jerusalem, the Arctic and, of course, College Green. Wherever we've gone, the #PuzzleForToday has gone too.

Our regular series of broadcasts from the UK's leading universities has thrown up an exciting new cast of puzzle-writing characters. It's an important component of the #PuzzleForToday that it should be owned by our listeners and contributors, rather than professional puzzlers, and it's been fun to watch as they read them out in front of a live audience of their students and colleagues.

I'm particularly proud of the Arctic puzzles which feature in Chapter 6. We asked for one to mark the fact that that we would be broadcasting from Ny-Alesund on Svalbard in March 2019. Who would have thought that we would hit on such a rich vein of puzzling enthusiasm amidst the sea ice and glaciers at the top of the world?

Inevitably, though, that has meant a lot of maths. I've tried to corral these into 'Practical' and 'Further' maths, separating those that seemed to have a real-world application from the harder puzzles. Another way of thinking about them might be 'Applied' and 'Pure' or even just 'Easy' and 'Hard'. At some level, all puzzles are mathematical, in that they demand you work something out, but you shouldn't need a slide rule or a calculator until you get to Chapter 4.

We've really enjoyed the way that the *Today* programme presenters have begun to seep into the texture of the puzzles. It's one thing to substitute the name John, Mishal, Justin, Nick or Martha for person 'A' or person 'B', but quite another to introduce elements of their character or personal foibles that come across on the radio. Maybe that should come as no surprise since we all have breakfast with them every day. No surprise either that so many puzzles feature alarm clocks. And coffee, lots of coffee.

And for next year? As Douglas Adams said, 'predicting the future is a mug's game'. Who thought that, towards the end of 2019, we'd still be obsessing over the Withdrawal Agreement? If I have to though, I'll hazard a guess that climate change, biodiversity loss and our relationship with Artificial Intelligence will all be major themes in the year to come. Get puzzling.

Tom Feilden, Science & Environment Editor on the *Today* programme

# CHAPTER 1

# EVERYDAY

# ENIGMAS

All human life is here. And quite a lot of animal, plant, bacteriological and artificial life, with a sprinkling of magic fairy dust and some poetry thrown in for good measure.

If you're new to #PuzzleForToday, this is the place to start. It's mostly logic and common sense (thinking about Archimedes and his bath may help), and where there is some maths it's fairly straightforward. If you break the puzzles down and take each step in turn you should get there.

Hitch a ride on one of the flying carpets and flit around picking the puzzles that catch your eye, but be careful which magic carpet company you fly with.

**1**  The Royal Albert Hall is a large auditorium with an internal volume of about 100,000m$^3$. The air in the hall weighs 120 tonnes. If the concentration of $CO_2$ in the atmosphere rises to 400 parts per million, how much $CO_2$ is there in the Albert Hall?

*Hugh Hunt, Reader in Engineering Dynamics and Vibration at Trinity College, Cambridge*

**2**  I'm doing the washing up and a 400ml empty glass jar is floating in the water. The jar weighs 300g when empty. How much water do I need to pour into the floating jar to make it sink? Assume that the density of glass is three times the density of water.

*Hugh Hunt, Reader in Engineering Dynamics and Vibration at Trinity College, Cambridge*

**3**  At the station, I usually stand on the escalator and the ride takes 30 seconds from bottom to top. Sometimes the escalator is not working and it takes me 60 seconds to climb up the stationary steps. On days when I feel like walking up the moving escalator I count 40 steps.

How many steps are there on the escalator?

*Hugh Hunt, Reader in Engineering Dynamics and Vibration at Trinity College, Cambridge*

**4**    A miserly mathematician reckons:

**Five 2p coins are equivalent to ten 1p coins**

**Ten 10p coins are equivalent to twenty 5p coins**

**Five 50p coins are equivalent to eight 20p coins.**

What were they thinking of?

*School of Mathematics and Statistics at the University of Sheffield*

**5**    When I blow across the top of an empty glass bottle I get a low note and when I tap the side of the bottle with a spoon the note is high.

When the bottle is half full of water, the note I blow gets higher and the note from tapping with a spoon gets lower.

Why does one note go up and the other go down?

*Hugh Hunt, Reader in Engineering Dynamics and Vibration at Trinity College, Cambridge*

**6** I'm in an elevator. On the floor is a bowl of water with an apple floating in it. Hovering in front of me is a perfectly balanced helium balloon. Hanging from the ceiling of the elevator is a bag of sand suspended by a rubber band.

When the elevator accelerates upwards, does the apple sink or rise in the water?

What does the helium balloon do?

What happens to the bag of sand?

*Hugh Hunt, Reader in Engineering Dynamics and Vibration at Trinity College, Cambridge*

**7** For today's puzzle, the presenter reads out four whole numbers and asks you to add them. You are in a rush and mishear the puzzle, multiplying the numbers instead. However, you get the answer right. Which four numbers were read out?

*Kyle D Evans (@kyledevans) is an award-winning maths communicator and Head of Maths at Barton Peveril College www.kyledevans.com*

**8** My alarm clock shows the time as four digits. One night, I set the clock but accidentally place it upside down on my bedside table. In the morning I don't notice anything. What time do I get up?

*Kyle D Evans (@kyledevans) is an award-winning maths communicator and Head of Maths at Barton Peveril College www.kyledevans.com*

**9**   When I first wake up, I can never remember if my bedside calendar gives dates in British format (day/month/year) or American (month/day/year). How many days a year might I be confused by this?

*Kyle D Evans (@kyledevans) is an award-winning maths communicator and Head of Maths at Barton Peveril College www.kyledevans.com*

**10**   What was special about twenty-six minutes to one on 5 June 1978?

*Dr Lynda White, Department of Mathematics, Imperial College London*

**11**   What is happening in this riddle?

*With seven to share,*
*Between five, then it's fair,*
*To begin by each taking one.*
*But then: a surprise!*
*Because then there lies*
*The remainder, of which there is none.*

*The Maths Department, Oxford High School GDST*

**12**　For the NHS's 70th birthday celebrations, some Cambridge primary school students have drawn the letters spelling HAPPY BIRTHDAY on individual A4 sheets to send to Addenbrooke's Hospital in Cambridge. There are five sheets for the word HAPPY and eight sheets for the word BIRTHDAY. Unfortunately, the student carrying the sheets drops the pile of papers that spell the word HAPPY.

Assuming the student doesn't look at the sheets, what is the probability that they will pick up those five pieces of paper in the right order to spell HAPPY?

*Bobby Seagull (@bobby_seagull) is a school maths teacher and doctorate student in Mathematics Education at Cambridge University. www.bobbyseagull.com*

**13**　2018 saw the 80th anniversary of the first publication of *Beano* magazine. To celebrate, Dennis the Menace had a race against Minnie the Minx.

Dennis was sneaky and gave himself a head start, setting off at midday and travelling at an average speed of 10km/h.

Minnie started 30 minutes later and travelled at an average speed of 15km/h.

At what time did she catch up with Dennis?

*Bobby Seagull (@bobby_seagull) is a school maths teacher and doctorate student in Mathematics Education at Cambridge University. www.bobbyseagull.com*

**14**   Chris and Kem, stars of *Love Island 2017*, hosted a watching party for the latest series final. They asked their friends to select their favourite party drink out of four options: lemonade, champagne, wine and ginger beer.

20% chose lemonade, 15% chose champagne and 30% chose wine.

If 24 friends chose wine, how many people chose ginger beer?

*Bobby Seagull (@bobby_seagull) is a school maths teacher and doctorate student in Mathematics Education at Cambridge University. www.bobbyseagull.com*

**15**   Two school teachers, Camille and Nicole, are preparing a party to celebrate Thanksgiving.

They spend one-fifth of the time baking snacks. They spend one-third of the time making drinks. They spend the remaining time, 70 minutes, tidying their flat.

How long did Camille and Nicole spend preparing in total?

*Bobby Seagull (@bobby_seagull) is a school maths teacher and doctorate student in Mathematics Education at Cambridge University. www.bobbyseagull.com*

**16** Write down the answers to the following two clues.

**Clue 1:** What short word means to be in a position in which the lower part of the body is resting on a seat?

**Clue 2:** What is the plural of the geological phenomenon that occurs when hot materials from the Earth's interior are thrown out of a volcano?

Now, what Halloween-themed word can you create using all the letters from the answers?

*Bobby Seagull (@bobby_seagull) is a school maths teacher and doctorate student in Mathematics Education at Cambridge University. www.bobbyseagull.com*

**17** A student buys a new school uniform set for £100, which includes a 20 per cent discount. What was the original price before the discount?

*Bobby Seagull (@bobby_seagull) is a school maths teacher and doctorate student in Mathematics Education at Cambridge University. www.bobbyseagull.com*

**18** Does there exist a natural number whose letters appear in alphabetical order when spelt out?

*School of Mathematics and Statistics at the University of Sheffield*

**19** Nelson's Column in Trafalgar Square was unveiled in 1843. On a twist to a classic problem, if it takes five robotic builders five minutes to make five of Nelson's hats, how long would it take 100 robotic builders to make 100 of Nelson's hats? (Warning: Don't follow your gut for this puzzle!)

*Bobby Seagull (@bobby_seagull) is a school maths teacher and doctorate student in Mathematics Education at Cambridge University. www.bobbyseagull.com*

**20** The United Nations officially came into existence on 24 October 1945. The original plans to celebrate in the capital cities of the five permanent members of the Security Council had to be postponed. Instead, parties were held in the capitals of the following countries: Portugal, New Zealand, Liberia, Argentina and Cambodia.

Apart from their geographic spread, why were these capital cities appropriate replacements?

*Bobby Seagull (@bobby_seagull) is a school maths teacher and doctorate student in Mathematics Education at Cambridge University. www.bobbyseagull.com*

**21**  On the day of the Nobel Prize awards ceremony, a primary school class bakes circular mince pies in the design of a Nobel medal.

They cut each mince pie into three parts. The first portion is a quarter of the pie. The second portion is a third of the pie.

In degrees, what is the angle of the remaining final portion of the mince pie?

*Bobby Seagull (@bobby_seagull) is a school maths teacher and doctorate student in Mathematics Education at Cambridge University. www.bobbyseagull.com*

**22**  The first ever lottery draw in England was held in 1569 to raise money for Queen Elizabeth I's Royal Navy and foreign exploration. The first modern National Lottery was held in 1994.

Players had to select six numbers between 1 and 49. They would win the jackpot if their six choices matched the six numbered balls picked randomly by the lottery machine.

What was the probability of a player picking the six correct numbers?

*Bobby Seagull (@bobby_seagull) is a school maths teacher and doctorate student in Mathematics Education at Cambridge University. www.bobbyseagull.com*

**23**   A primary school child creates a simple model of the Solar System showing the three inner planets: Mercury, Venus and Earth. The model shows perfect circular orbits and all planets are aligned at the start of year.

We assume that Mercury takes a quarter of an earth-year and Venus two-thirds of an earth-year to make one complete orbit of the Sun at the centre.

How long would it take for all three planets to align again in the same position that they started?

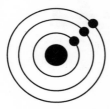

*Bobby Seagull (@bobby_seagull) is a school maths teacher and doctorate student in Mathematics Education at Cambridge University. www.bobbyseagull.com*

**24**   In the final of the Explore Learning National Young Mathematicians of the Year at the University of Cambridge, teams of four students test their mathematical wits to be crowned primary and secondary school champions.

If one winning team of four students does a high-five with every other team mate, how many high-fives will there be?

*Bobby Seagull (@bobby_seagull) is a school maths teacher and doctorate student in Mathematics Education at Cambridge University. www.bobbyseagull.com*

**25** To celebrate the start of the Chinese New Year in 2019 as the Year of the Pig, siblings Peter and Layla buy some animal-shaped sweets. They choose some cheaper dog-shaped sweets as the Year of the Dog was 2018, and some pricier pig-shaped sweets.

Peter buys four pig sweets and two dog sweets for £9.

Layla buys two pig sweets and two dog sweets for £5.

How much do the pig-shaped and dog-shaped sweets costs individually?

**Peter**

**Layla**

*Bobby Seagull (@bobby_seagull) is a school maths teacher and doctorate student in Mathematics Education at Cambridge University. www.bobbyseagull.com*

**26**   As a hint, this puzzle would be called 'The One With Cryptic Clues'.

A prophetic Greek deity, a German steed, a Jewish matriarch, the patron saint of married women, and a candle keeper walk into a coffee shop. A young animal is missing – what is it?

*David Baynard (www.baynard.dev) is finishing a PhD in biotechnology at Emmanuel College, Cambridge*


## 27   GUSHARON'S GARDEN

Gusharon owns a large fairy garden. She has sown 4,000 fairy flower bulbs, split equally between blue, yellow, red and purple flowers.

Unfortunately, Gusharon's garden is infested with the infamous fairy flatworm. The bulbs have different levels of resistance to the worm. Yellow bulbs are three times as likely to be eaten as blue bulbs. Red bulbs are half as likely to be eaten as yellow bulbs and the purple bulbs are five times more likely to be eaten as red bulbs.

Gusharon's gardener tells her she should expect 2,700 bulbs to flower this year. How will this be split between the different colours?

*Sally Calder, Education Actuary, Institute and Faculty of Actuaries*


**28**   Is it possible to express 2018 as a sum of consecutive whole numbers?

*School of Mathematics and Statistics at the University of Sheffield*

## 29 SPIDER POPULATION

A scientist is studying a particular species of spider. Research on spider life expectancy shows that 99 out of every 100 newly hatched spiders will survive the first day, 98 out of every 100 one-day-old spiders survive a second day, 97 out of every 100 two-day old spiders survive a third day and so on, with the survival probability falling each day.

It's the first day of the month and the scientist has just taken a delivery of 10,000 newly hatched spiders for his research. His supervisor has told him he'll only get funding for his research if at least 100 spiders are still alive by the first day of the next month.

Will he get his funding?

*Sally Calder, Education Actuary, Institute and Faculty of Actuaries*

## 30

Is it possible to cut a strip of ribbon 27cm long from a strip that is 144cm long without using a tape measure?

*School of Mathematics and Statistics at the University of Sheffield*

## 31 SOFT LANDING

A magic airport services two flying carpet companies, Flying Rug and Soaring Mat. Carpets fray very easily and undergo a safety inspection after each landing. If a carpet fails an inspection it's taken out of service for repairs.

Flying Rug fails two out of every ten landing inspections.

Soaring Mat fails eight out of every ten inspections.

There are 30 landings expected today: 20 from Flying Rug and 10 from Soaring Mat.

One of the carpet inspectors is enjoying his morning tea break when his colleague tells him that the first carpet has just landed and has failed the inspection.

What is the chance that this carpet was from Soaring Mat?

*Sally Calder, Education Actuary, Institute and Faculty of Actuaries*

## 32

It is the future, and the public debt has risen to the 300-digit number obtained by writing down the numbers 100 to 199 one after another.

The Chancellor of the Exchequer decides to add all the digits of this number. What number do they find?

*School of Mathematics and Statistics at the University of Sheffield*

## 33  EXAM SUCCESS

In a particular school, students wanting to join the actuarial science class have to pass two examinations – statistics and finance.

Students passing both on the first attempt are admitted straight into the class and students failing both on the first attempt are immediately disqualified.

Students who pass one and fail the other are given one attempt to re-sit the one they failed and are admitted into the class if they pass it on the second attempt. They are disqualified if they fail it again.

Four in ten students are expected to pass both exams on the first attempt. One in ten are expected to fail both.

Of the students who fail one exam on their first attempt, it's equally likely to be statistics or finance. Three out of four students who re-sit statistics pass it and half of those who re-sit finance pass.

A student is about to sit the exams for the first time. What is the overall chance that she'll be admitted into the class?

*Sally Calder, Education Actuary, Institute and Faculty of Actuaries*

**34**  I am thinking of a number between 1 and 32. Can you determine the number by asking no more than five questions with yes/no answers?

*School of Mathematics and Statistics at the University of Sheffield*

**35** On your commute to work you travel at an average speed of 30mph. You take exactly the same route home but average a speed of 90mph.

What was your average speed on your commute to and from work?

*School of Mathematics and Statistics at the University of Sheffield*

**36** You are blindfolded and put in front of a table with four coins on it. Exactly two of the coins on the table are heads-up. Without taking your blindfold off, how can you rearrange the coins into two piles that both have the same number of coins showing heads?

*School of Mathematics and Statistics at the University of Sheffield*

**37** Your friend's pension fund consists of £1 in cash and £99 in tulip bulbs. One morning they hear, on the *Today* programme, about a crash in the price of tulip bulbs. They immediately phone their broker who tells them that their tulip bulbs now only make up 98 per cent of their pension fund.

How much is your friend's pension fund now worth?

*School of Mathematics and Statistics at the University of Sheffield*

## 38 GOING AROUND IN CIRCLES

The Yamanote Line in Tokyo is a railway loop with 29 stations. In one of the stations, I find trains waiting to go in each direction. I want to go two stations clockwise, but due to industrial action the drivers are only stopping at every eleventh station.

Which train should I get on – clockwise or anticlockwise?

*School of Mathematics and Statistics at the University of Sheffield*

## 39

It would take you a year to build a shrine in honour of the *Today* programme on your own. However, your partner builds at the same speed as you, your three children and their 99 friends build half as quickly as you, and your parents can each build twice as quickly as you but half as quickly as their parents.

How long would it take all 110 of you to build the shrine if it's not a leap year?

*School of Mathematics and Statistics at the University of Sheffield*

**40**  One hundred lemmings are placed on a long levitating steel beam. Each lemming faces one of the two ends of the beam. All the lemmings walk at the same constant speed in the direction they are facing. If two lemmings bump into each other, they both turn and walk in the opposite direction.

Are all the lemmings guaranteed to fall off the beam?

*School of Mathematics and Statistics at the University of Sheffield*

**41**  Sabine has an electric car. She embarks on a 420-mile journey. The car has a range of 210 miles, travels at 70mph and takes 45 minutes to recharge.

Chris has a diesel car with a range in excess of 420 miles when travelling at 60mph.

I arrive first. Who am I?

**Diesel**
420 miles at 60mph

**Electric**
420 miles at 70mph

*Dr Shaun Fitzgerald, Director of the Royal Institution*

**42**    The DNA code takes the form of four possible letters (ATGC) arranged in a three-letter word. The code word for 'start making protein' is ATG and for 'stop making protein' the code word is TAG.

If any two letters of the start code are mutated, what is the probability that the start signal becomes stop?

*Dr Shaun Fitzgerald, Director of the Royal Institution*

**43**    I have four sons and one nephew. My sons are as close to me genetically as my nephew. How can this be?

*Dr Shaun Fitzgerald, Director of the Royal Institution*

## 44 SHEEP SHEARING

Heather and Dylan are sheep. It takes a shepherd three minutes to shear Heather's fleece. Dylan, being a sizeable ram, is twice as wide as Heather. Assuming, as all good scientists do, that all animals are spherical, how long should it take the shepherd to shear Dylan?

*Dr Geoff Evatt, School of Mathematics, University of Manchester*

## 45 CHOCOLATE RAID

A girl creeps downstairs precisely six minutes before her parents wake up, to secretly raid her pile of Easter eggs.

Within the pile are:

six small eggs, which take one minute each to eat,
three medium-sized eggs, which take two minutes each to eat,
and two large eggs, which take three minutes each to eat.

Given a medium egg is twice the weight of a small egg, and a large egg is twice the weight of a medium egg, what is the girl's optimal strategy for consuming as much chocolate as possible without being caught?

*Dr Geoff Evatt, School of Mathematics, University of Manchester*

**46**  My friend puts three identical pairs of gloves in a box and jumbles them up.

I pick out two gloves at random.

What is the probability that I now have a left glove and a right glove?

*School of Mathematics and Statistics at the University of Sheffield*

## 47  DUCKLINGS VERSUS FOX

Claire owns some ducks, and notices that their large clutch of 24 eggs is beginning to hatch.

She decides to give them some space and return three hours later.

The ducklings hatch out at a steady rate of eight eggs per hour.

However, at the end of each hour a fox visits the clutch and eats half of the hatched ducklings.

How many ducklings does Claire discover upon her return?

*Dr Geoff Evatt, School of Mathematics, University of Manchester*

## 48 THREE HENS AND ONE OMELETTE

Iris owns three hens: Tilly, Olivia and Gillian. Each week

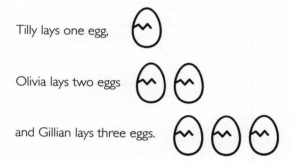

Tilly lays one egg,

Olivia lays two eggs

and Gillian lays three eggs.

At the end of the week, Iris gathers up all six eggs and randomly selects three of them to cook herself an omelette. What is the probability that each hen has contributed to the omelette?

*Dr Geoff Evatt, School of Mathematics, University of Manchester*

# CHAPTER 2

# PEOPLE, PLACES AND GETTING THERE

From leaves on the line to Pink Floyd, it pays to know your celebrities – and how and where to find them.

There's something for the geographer here, for the astronomer, the poet and the historian. It's all about the planes, trains and automobiles that connect them.

**49** After a heavy storm, debris needs to be cleared from several train lines. A crew is sent to clear the following lines:

**Brighton – Worthing – Horsham**

**Horsham – Three Bridges – Redhill**

**Redhill – Dorking – Horsham**

**Three Bridges – Haywards Heath – Brighton**

What route should they take to ensure they only go through each track once (i.e. they don't traverse the same track twice) without exiting any stations?

HINT: From which of these locations does the crew need to start cleaning?

*Dr Nicos Georgiou, Senior Lecturer in Mathematics at the University of Sussex*

**50** To celebrate what would have been Roald Dahl's birthday, four of his book characters have been invited to a special party.

The first is the champion of the world.

The second is the tortoise in *Esio Trot*.

The third is the teacher who befriended Matilda.

The fourth is Matilda's best school friend.

Why have these four characters been invited?

*Bobby Seagull (@bobby_seagull) is a school maths teacher and doctorate student in Mathematics Education at Cambridge University. www.bobbyseagull.com*

**51**  Assume the Moon is a mathematically perfect sphere. If its radius was doubled, how many times larger would the new volume be?

*Bobby Seagull (@bobby_seagull) is a school maths teacher and doctorate student in Mathematics Education at Cambridge University. www.bobbyseagull.com*

**52**  In 2018 we celebrated the 280th anniversary of the birth of William Herschel, the German-born British astronomer who discovered the planet Uranus.

Imagine you had a rope that wrapped around Uranus's 160,000-km equator. Based on a classic problem, if you put one-metre high sticks right around the equator and lay the rope on top, how much longer does the rope need to be make ends meet?

(Note that as Uranus is a gas-based planet, this might be a tricky experiment to carry out in real life!)

*Bobby Seagull (@bobby_seagull) is a school maths teacher and doctorate student in Mathematics Education at Cambridge University. www.bobbyseagull.com*

**53**  To mark what would have been the birthday of American lyricist Alan Jay Lerner – renowned for his work on *My Fair Lady* and *An American in Paris* – a mathematically-minded conductor requests an unusually sequenced orchestra to perform in Lerner's memory.

The orchestra has:

**I piano**
**I trumpet**
**2 flutes**
**3 cellos**
**5 flutes**
**8 French horns**
**and 13 violas.**

How many violins are there to complete this mathematically sequenced orchestra?

*Bobby Seagull (@bobby_seagull) is a school maths teacher and doctorate student in Mathematics Education at Cambridge University. www.bobbyseagull.com*

**54**  Louise Brown, the world's first IVF or 'test-tube' baby turned 40 in 2018. For her birthday celebrations, Louise invited five close friends, but could only choose three to join her for a cocktail-making class.

How many different groupings of three friends could she select?

*Bobby Seagull (@bobby_seagull) is a school maths teacher and doctorate student in Mathematics Education at Cambridge University. www.bobbyseagull.com*

**55**  The United Nation's World Population Day was established to raise awareness of global population issues.

The global population may reach ten billion as early as 2038. If the annual percentage growth rate for the population is the same every year for the next 20 years, what would the annual percentage rate be for the 2018 population of 7.6 billion to reach 10 billion by 2038?

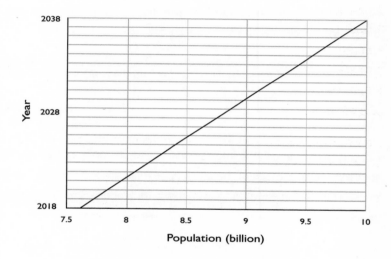

*Bobby Seagull (@bobby_seagull) is a school maths teacher and doctorate student in Mathematics Education at Cambridge University. www.bobbyseagull.com*

**56**  From Singapore, I fly ten hours due west to Equatorial Guinea – a distance of 10,000km. From there I fly ten hours due north.

How long is my flight from there back to Singapore?

*Hugh Hunt, Reader in Engineering Dynamics and Vibration at Trinity College, Cambridge*

**57**  Alexander Fleming discovered penicillin at St Mary's Hospital, London, by noticing mould developing accidentally on some culture dishes.

At the start of day one, mould sample A weighs 1g and increases in weight by 20 per cent each day compounded.

Equivalently, mould sample B weighs 2g and increases in weight by 10 per cent each day compounded.

After how many days is sample A heavier than sample B? Assume that the growth happens at the end of each day.

*Bobby Seagull (@bobby_seagull) is a school maths teacher and doctorate student in Mathematics Education at Cambridge University. www.bobbyseagull.com*

**58**  On one particular day, the International Space Station is a bright, visible spot moving over much of the UK. It appears at around 8:25pm, low in the western sky, and moves towards the east. It appears to be travelling at about the same speed as a brightly lit passenger plane.

We know that planes typically fly at a speed of 900km/h at a height of 10km. The space station is at a height of 300km. Roughly how fast is it going?

Earth's circumference is about 40,000km. How long does it take for the Space Station to make one orbit of Earth?

*Hugh Hunt, Reader in Engineering Dynamics and Vibration at Trinity College, Cambridge*

**59** Tyger tyger burning bright, can you get this puzzle right?

On a particular day, poet, printmaker and painter William Blake spent 40 per cent of the working day writing poetry, a quarter of the day printmaking and the remaining 3.5 hours on painting.

How long was his working day?

*Bobby Seagull (@bobby_seagull) is a school maths teacher and doctorate student in Mathematics Education at Cambridge University. www.bobbyseagull.com*

**60** 19 January 2019 saw the 600th anniversary of a major event in the Hundred Years' War. English forces loyal to Henry V captured Rouen, the capital of Normandy, from the Norman French.

The English contingent was 2.5 times larger than the French one.

If the total combined English and French forces were 14,000, how many were on each side?

*Bobby Seagull (@bobby_seagull) is a school maths teacher and doctorate student in Mathematics Education at Cambridge University. www.bobbyseagull.com*

**61** Roadworks on the motorway are slowing my journey. I drive at 30mph for ten miles and then at 60mph for another ten miles.

What is my average speed over this 20-mile stretch of motorway?

*Hugh Hunt, Reader in Engineering Dynamics and Vibration at Trinity College, Cambridge*

**62**   It's the winter solstice and the midday shadows are at their longest.

There's a flagpole in the park near my house, and today it will cast a noonday shadow that's 40m long. The lunchtime shadow in midsummer will be only 5.6m long. How tall is the flagpole?

40m                                                     5.6m

*Hugh Hunt, Reader in Engineering Dynamics and Vibration at Trinity College, Cambridge*

**63**   On the occasion of her Official Birthday in June 2019, Queen Elizabeth II celebrated her 93rd birthday.

What is special about the number formed by adding up all the factors of Her Majesty's age?

*Dr Shaun Fitzgerald, Director of the Royal Institution*

**64**  As lorries get heavier, road bridges have to be strengthened – at great cost. An engineer has proposed instead that freight be shifted onto barges using Britain's extensive canal network. She knows that there are many bridges that carry canals over railways and roads, but she argues that there is no need to strengthen canal bridges even for the heaviest of barges.

How can this be so?

*Hugh Hunt, Reader in Engineering Dynamics and Vibration at Trinity College, Cambridge*

**65**  I'm late for my flight. It's a ten-minute walk to the gate but fortunately there are moving walkways for about half the journey. I'm not much of a runner but I'll try to do about one minute of running.

I want to get to my gate as quickly as possible, so should I do that little bit of running on the moving walkway or is it better to run on the bits in between?

*Hugh Hunt, Reader in Engineering Dynamics and Vibration at Trinity College, Cambridge*

**66**  Early this morning there was a fresh dusting of snow. On the road I saw the wobbly tracks from a bicycle. The tracks from each wheel were clearly visible, criss-crossing back and forth over each other.

Can I tell from the tracks which direction the cyclist was riding?

*Hugh Hunt, Reader in Engineering Dynamics and Vibration at Trinity College, Cambridge*

**67**   Let's make the approximation that Venus, Earth and Mars move on circular orbits of radius 2, 3 and 4 respectively.

To the nearest 10 per cent, what is the proportion of time that Mars spends closer to the Earth than Venus?

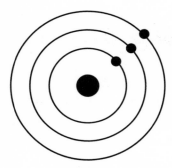

*Hugh Hunt, Reader in Engineering Dynamics and Vibration at Trinity College, Cambridge*

**68**   The SS *Great Britain* was the longest passenger ship in the world when she was launched from Bristol on 19 July 1843.

The cost to tour the ship today is £63 for three adults and two children. It is £48 for two adults and two children.

What would it cost for one adult and one child?

*Bobby Seagull (@bobby_seagull) is a school maths teacher and doctorate student in Mathematics Education at Cambridge University. www.bobbyseagull.com*

**69**  My vintage aircraft has three engines, each with a 20 per cent chance of failing on a given flight.

What are the odds of losing only one engine?

And the odds that all three will fail?

*Hugh Hunt, Reader in Engineering Dynamics and Vibration at Trinity College, Cambridge*

**70**  Sir Walter Mildmay served as Chancellor of the Exchequer for Queen Elizabeth I, and founded Emmanuel College at Cambridge University in 1584.

Write out the letters in the name Walter Mildmay. Now cross out a letter each time they appear in the country whose capital city is Valletta and the surname of the actor who portrayed Willy Wonka in 1971.

With the two remaining uncrossed letters, what country's two-letter ISO code can be written?

*Bobby Seagull (@bobby_seagull) is a school maths teacher and doctorate student in Mathematics Education at Cambridge University. www.bobbyseagull.com*

# CHAPTER 3

# PRACTICAL

## MATHS

The puzzles here are all about problem solving. Don't be fooled, they're easier than they look.

If you don't know the mathematical formulas, you can usually work backwards using logic, trial and error, and a bit of brute force with your fingers. We'll start with some easy ones to get you going.

**71**   Humphrys High has 207 students, with an equal number in each class. How many classes are there, with how many students in each?

*Kyle D Evans (@kyledevans) is an award-winning maths communicator and Head of Maths at Barton Peveril College www.kyledevans.com*

**72**   In the First Lego League in Cambridge, students programmed three robots to take part in the Robot Games. The robots picked up Lego bricks at different speeds, simulating a Mars space-probe lander picking up debris from the surface of the planet.

Robot A picked up twice as many bricks as Robot B, and
Robot A picked up four more than Robot C.
In total, the robots picked up 36 bricks.

How many did Robot A pick up?

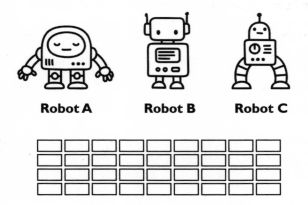

**Robot A**      **Robot B**      **Robot C**

*Bobby Seagull (@bobby_seagull) is a school maths teacher and doctorate student in Mathematics Education at Cambridge University. www.bobbyseagull.com*

**73** Ahead of A-Level results day, a group of students is preparing to celebrate. Their teacher sets them a classic maths puzzle. Because the students like jelly beans, the teacher gives them regular A4 paper to create the sides of the cylinder that will hold the celebratory jelly beans.

Assuming that they don't need to make the base or lid of the container, will they get more volume in the cylinder by curving the A4 paper along its shorter side or its longer side?

*Bobby Seagull (@bobby_seagull) is a school maths teacher and doctorate student in Mathematics Education at Cambridge University. www.bobbyseagull.com*

**74** It is GCSE results day. Three of Mr Seagull's maths students, Naga, Tim and Jayne, have a joint five-digit code that can be used to unlock their GCSE results envelope.

The catch is that each student only has one part of the code.

Naga has the number 7, Tim has the number 3 and Jayne has the number 19, so the first four digits of the code are 7 – 3 – 19.

Bobby holds the fifth and final number that will unlock the GCSE code. What is his number?

*Bobby Seagull (@bobby_seagull) is a school maths teacher and doctorate student in Mathematics Education at Cambridge University. www.bobbyseagull.com*

**75** Kristoff the Koala is waiting for an important delivery. To pass the time, he writes down all the numbers from one to ten thousand on the same line, without leaving any gaps between the digits.

When he has finished, in how many places will it appear that he has written 2018?

*Daniel Griller: teacher and author of*
Elastic Numbers *and* Problem Solving in GCSE Mathematics

**76** Mr and Mrs Indigo and their two children meet Mr and Mrs Violet and their two children at the cinema.

In how many ways can the eight of them arrange themselves in a single row of eight seats, so that each of them is seated next to a member of their own family?

*Daniel Griller: teacher and author of*
Elastic Numbers *and* Problem Solving in GCSE Mathematics

**77** Lucy the Labrador is playing with square tiles of side length one. She arranges them into a rectangle (with one side longer than the other), and notices that the area and perimeter are equal.

How many tiles did she use?

*Daniel Griller: teacher and author of*
Elastic Numbers *and* Problem Solving in GCSE Mathematics

**78**  Confronting two liars and two truth-tellers, Steven boomed, 'Alright — who ate the last cupcake?!'

'Wasn't me,' said Angelina.

'Yes it was!' protested Brad.

'It was Brad or Dustin,' said Charlize.

'Definitely Brad,' claimed Dustin.

Who was the cupcake-consuming culprit?

*Daniel Griller: teacher and author of*
**Elastic Numbers** *and* **Problem Solving in GCSE Mathematics**

**79**  There is a number on a computer screen, and two buttons that can be pressed. Button X quarters the number shown and button Y subtracts 9 from the number shown.

Olivia presses button X, then button Y, then X, then Y, and so on, until each button has been pressed ten times.

The final number shown is the same as the original number. What is this number?

*Daniel Griller: teacher and author of*
**Elastic Numbers** *and* **Problem Solving in GCSE Mathematics**

**80** Find three numbers that come next to each other and which add up to 30.

*David Feather – a mathematics education lecturer for some time at the University of the West of England, the University of Wales, Newport and the Open University*

**81** A boy has twice as much money as his friend. If they have 84p together, how much does each have?

*David Feather – a mathematics education lecturer for some time at the University of the West of England, the University of Wales, Newport and the Open University*

**82** Two ice creams are eaten by two children in two minutes. How long will it take five children to eat five ice creams?

*David Feather – a mathematics education lecturer for some time at the University of the West of England, the University of Wales, Newport and the Open University*

**83** A girl is five years older than her brother. If the sum of their ages is 17, how old are they?

*David Feather – a mathematics education lecturer for some time at the University of the West of England, the University of Wales, Newport and the Open University*

**84**   A lady has a 3-litre jug and a 5-litre jug. Using only these jugs and water from a tap, how can she measure exactly 1 litre of water?

*David Feather – a mathematics education lecturer for some time at the University of the West of England, the University of Wales, Newport and the Open University*

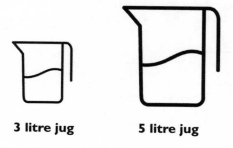

**3 litre jug**       **5 litre jug**

**85**   An electric train is travelling due north. If the wind is blowing from the north-west, in which direction is the smoke blowing?

*David Feather – a mathematics education lecturer for some time at the University of the West of England, the University of Wales, Newport and the Open University*

**86**   In an election, one man got 32 more votes than his opponent. If the total of their votes was 318, how many did each get?

*David Feather – a mathematics education lecturer for some time at the University of the West of England, the University of Wales, Newport and the Open University*

**87**  With 12 square tiles, you can make 3 different rectangles that use all the tiles without leaving any gaps.

Find the smallest number of tiles required to make four different rectangles.

What is the smallest number of square tiles needed to make five different rectangles?

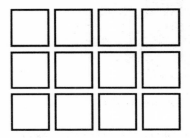

*David Feather – a mathematics education lecturer for some time at the University of the West of England, the University of Wales, Newport and the Open University*

**88**  Two children want to buy a packet of sweets. They both have some money, but one is 24p short of the price and the other 2p short.

When they put their money together, they still don't have enough to buy the packet of sweets.

How much money does each child have?

*David Feather – a mathematics education lecturer for some time at the University of the West of England, the University of Wales, Newport and the Open University*

**89** Glasgow and London are 400 miles apart.

A train leaves Glasgow at 11:00 for London and averages a speed of 80mph.

Another train leaves London for Glasgow at 10:30 and averages 70mph.

Which train is nearer London when they cross?

**Glasgow train**          **London Train**

*David Feather – a mathematics education lecturer for some time at the University of the West of England, the University of Wales, Newport and the Open University*

**90** I've just taken part in a race.

If one more person had beaten me, there would have been the same number of people in front of me as there were behind me.

If one more had been behind me, there would have been three times as many behind as in front.

How many people took part in the race and what was my finishing position?

*David Feather – a mathematics education lecturer for some time at the University of the West of England, the University of Wales, Newport and the Open University*

**91**   A mother and her son have £22 between them.

The mother and her daughter have £20 between them.

The son and daughter have £15 between them.

How much money does each have?

*David Feather – a mathematics education lecturer for some time at the University of the West of England, the University of Wales, Newport and the Open University*

**92**   A monster has been discovered which grows at such a rate that it doubles in size every day.

If it is put in a box of volume $1\,m^3$ when it is born, it will completely fill the box after ten days.

How many days will it be before it fills half the box?

*David Feather – a mathematics education lecturer for some time at the University of the West of England, the University of Wales, Newport and the Open University*

**93**   On 5 November, a charity organised a special fireworks display.

There were five fireworks. When lit, you could see them rise from the ground as red streaks. Each one then split into 11 blue fireworks. Finally, each of these gave off 18 white flames.

How many different light trails did spectators see?

*Dr Shaun Fitzgerald, Director of the Royal Institution*

**94**    What is the angle between the hands of a clock at half past eleven?

*David Feather – a mathematics education lecturer for some time at the University of the West of England, the University of Wales, Newport and the Open University*

**95**    National Puzzle Day is on 29 January. In a special puzzle to honour the day, we ascribe the number 1 to the letter A, 2 to the letter B, and so on.

If you add up all the numbers from the letters in 'National Puzzle Day', then subtract the number formed by adding up the three numbers from the date it occurred in six-digit format, what is special about the number you end up with?

*Dr Shaun Fitzgerald, Director of the Royal Institution*

**96**    In 2018, the BBC reported on a large study from the University of Bristol. The study said that hip replacements are now so good that 89 per cent of them last 15 years. Similarly, 93 per cent of total knee replacements last the same time.

All things being equal, if you had both knees and both hips replaced, what is the implied probability that at least one of them would fail within 15 years?

*Dr Shaun Fitzgerald, Director of the Royal Institution*

**97**  A triangular-based pyramid, or tetrahedron, has four triangular sides and six edges.

Is it possible to slide your finger around all the edges once only without lifting your finger off? What about for a cube or an octahedron? And a dodecahedron and an icosahedron?

For only one of these is a finger-lift-free journey around the edges possible. Which one?

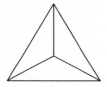

*Hugh Hunt, Reader in Engineering Dynamics and Vibration at Trinity College, Cambridge*

**98**  Five pirates of different ages have a treasure chest containing 100 gold coins. They decide to split the coins using a particular method. The oldest pirate proposes how to share the coins, and *all* pirates vote for or against it. If 50 per cent or more vote for it, the coins will be shared that way. Otherwise, the pirate proposing the scheme will be thrown overboard to be eaten by sharks, and the process will be repeated with the pirates that remain.

Assuming that all five pirates are intelligent, rational, greedy and do not wish to die (and are rather good at maths), what should the oldest pirate propose to save his life and get as many coins as he can?

*Dr Elon Correa, Lecturer in Mathematics and Statistics, University of Salford*

**99**  In an isosceles triangle, the size of the largest angle is four times that of the next largest angle.

What is the size of the largest angle?

*Hugh Hunt, Reader in Engineering Dynamics and Vibration at Trinity College, Cambridge*

## 100 RETIREMENT FUND

Susan is 45 years old and currently earns £50,000 a year. She plans to retire in 20 years' time at age 65. When she retires she would like to have an annual pension equal to one-half of her salary at age 65, payable for the rest of her life. She has inherited some money and would like to set aside enough now to cover the cost of the pension.

Susan's financial advisor, Bob, has told her that for a typical 65-year-old, £25 is needed to cover the cost of every £1 of annual pension. Bob has found an investment fund that he says will grow by 5 per cent each year and Susan expects her salary to increase by 3 per cent each year up to her retirement.

How much, to the nearest £5,000, should Susan set aside now to cover the cost of her pension?

*Sally Calder, Education Actuary, Institute and Faculty of Actuaries*

**101** At the Chipping Norton Literary Festival, there is a jumble sale for damaged books. One particular book has had two separate leaves torn out. The stall manager says that she can offer you the book for free if you can work out the torn page numbers. All you know is that the page numbers of the two missing leaves add up 82. What are the missing page numbers?

*Bobby Seagull (@bobby_seagull) is a school maths teacher and doctorate student in Mathematics Education at Cambridge University. www.bobbyseagull.com*

## 102 SID'S NEW CAR

Sid is saving up to buy a car in six years' time. He expects the car to cost £20,000 when he buys it, but he only has £14,000 in the bank.

Sid's friend Dave has told him about a special savings account where the money in the account will grow each year either by 7 per cent or by 3 per cent. In any one year the chance of the fund growing by 3 per cent is twice that of the fund growing by 7 per cent. The growth rate in any one year is not linked to the growth rate in any other year.

If Sid invests his money in the special account, what is the probability that he'll have enough to buy the car in six years' time?

*Sally Calder, Education Actuary, Institute and Faculty of Actuaries*

**103** A can of baked beans has a diameter of 7.6cm and a height of 11cm. Calculate the total surface area of the baked bean can to the nearest centimetre squared.

**Diameter**

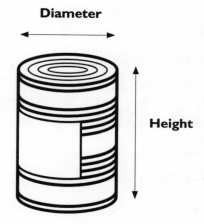

**Height**

*Bobby Seagull and fellow maths teacher Susan Okereke, co-hosts of the Maths Appeal podcast.*

**104** Maths Week London aims to change perceptions about maths as a subject and encourage all children, teachers and parents to share a love of maths.

In a Maths Week London event, there is a classroom-based session where there are twice as many children as parents and twice as many parents as teachers. If the room is full and the capacity is 35, how many children, parents and teachers are there?

*Bobby Seagull and fellow maths teacher Susan Okereke, co-hosts of the Maths Appeal podcast*

**105** Rachel and Bobby are hosting a party to celebrate National Numeracy Day for 20 National Numeracy supporters (including themselves). They want to make sure everyone attending has a glass of wine and a slice of pizza each. A bottle of wine costs £15 and fills five glasses, and a pizza costs £8 and can be cut into four slices.

Rachel has a mix-and-match '3 for 2' loyalty card with the cheapest item being free. Bobby has a voucher for 30% off. They cannot use both deals at once. Who should buy what, and what is the lowest price they can pay to make sure everyone is catered for?

*Bobby Seagull and Rachel Riley, from* Countdown. *Both are ambassadors for the National Numeracy charity and teamed up to celebrate National Numeracy Day.*

*Head to www.numeracyday.com to check your numeracy skills.*

**106** After 12 seasons, the American sitcom *The Big Bang Theory* aired its final episode in the UK in 2019. It initially centred around Caltech physicists Sheldon and Leonard and their interactions with their neighbour Penny. There are 279 episodes in total with each episode lasting 20 minutes.

A superfan wants to binge-watch the entire series. The superfan treats it as a job, watching Monday to Friday from 9am–5pm, with a one-hour lunch break. How many days would it take to complete the entire series?

*Bobby Seagull (@bobby_seagull) is a school maths teacher and doctorate student in Mathematics Education at Cambridge University. www.bobbyseagull.com*

**107** The radius of Circle A is a quarter the radius of Circle B.

Circle A rolls around Circle B once, and returns to its starting point.

How many revolutions will Circle A make in total?

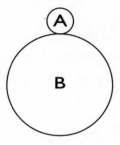

*Mr Ryan Glass, Teacher of Mathematics at Sevenoaks School*

## 108 AROUND THE U-BEND

I start a new toilet roll with a radius of 7cm, which decreases to 5cm when I have used half of it.

What is the radius of the cardboard tube in the middle?

*School of Mathematics and Statistics at the University of Sheffield*

# CHAPTER 4

## FURTHER

## MATHS

Don't be fooled by the water-pistol touting goblins or the references to children's games such as Snakes and Ladders – there's no getting away from the fact that these puzzles are a bit more challenging.

You'll need to know your algebra from your geometry and there's some mathematical terminology to get your head round. All I can say is good luck with the equilibrium distribution of a Markov chain.

**109** Dissatisfied politicians in both Blue and Red parties have decided to set up the Magenta party.

When a former member of the Blue party joins the Magentas, there is a 90 per cent chance that the next person to join will also be a former Blue.

When a former member of the Red party joins the Magentas, however, the chance is 75 per cent that the next new member will also be a former Red.

As the Magenta party grows, what is the proportion of members who used to belong to the Blue party?

*Dr Russell Gerrard, Associate Professor of Statistics, Faculty of Actuarial Science and Insurance,*
*Cass Business School*

**110** A fairground game involves rolling a die as many times as you want. You win if the total of all your rolls is a number you have chosen before you play.

What number should you choose?

*David Hargreaves, Visiting Lecturer, Faculty of Actuarial Science and Insurance,*
*Cass Business School*

**111** A maths professor invited a colleague to his home. As the two of them were walking there, the colleague said to the professor, 'Do you have any children?'

'Yes,' said the professor 'I have three daughters.'

The colleague said: 'What are their ages?'

The professor told him: 'The product of their ages is 36.'

The colleague replied: 'I cannot tell their ages from that.'

The professor then said: 'The sum of their ages is one more than the house we are passing.'

Again the colleague said: 'I cannot tell their ages from that.'

The professor then said: 'The eldest has just started piano lessons.'

And with that information, the colleague immediately knew their ages. What were they?

*Robin Michaelson, Visiting Lecturer, Faculty of Actuarial Science and Insurance, Cass Business School*

**112** In a land very far away, the annual rate of inflation is one million per cent. Assuming there are 365 days in a year, what is the daily rate of inflation?

*David Hargreaves, Visiting Lecturer, Faculty of Actuarial Science and Insurance, Cass Business School*

**113** Two brothers buy houses at the same time. They both borrow £250,000. The interest rates on the loans are 4 per cent when the outstanding amount is greater than £150,000 and 2 per cent when the outstanding amount is less than £150,000. (Interest is levied at the end of each year.)

Brother A repays £14,000 at the end of each year.

Brother B pays the interest at the end of each year (£10,000 = 4 per cent of £250,000) and then saves the other £4,000 in a savings account, with the intention of paying off the £250,000 loan in the future.

Both brothers end up paying off their loans in the same year.

What was the interest rate on brother B's savings account?

**A** Less than 2 per cent

**B** Between 2 per cent and 4 per cent

**C** Exactly 4 per cent

**D** More than 4 per cent

*David Hargreaves, Visiting Lecturer, Faculty of Actuarial Science and Insurance,*
*Cass Business School*

**114** A planet has three moons. They are currently all aligned and the closest moon will take one year to orbit the planet.

The middle moon is three times further from the closest moon than the closest moon is to the planet.

The furthest moon is five times as far away from the middle moon as the closest moon is from the planet.

How long will it be before all the moons are aligned again over the same spot on the planet? You can assume they all take circular orbits.

*David Hargreaves, Visiting Lecturer, Faculty of Actuarial Science and Insurance,*
*Cass Business School*

**115** A grid of squared paper measure 12 squares across by 8 squares down. If you draw a straight line from the top left-hand corner to the bottom right-hand corner, how many of the squares does the line cross?

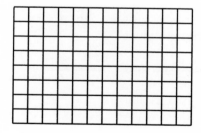

*David Hargreaves, Visiting Lecturer, Faculty of Actuarial Science and Insurance,*
*Cass Business School*

**116** An 18-year-old saves for his pension by putting £1,000 per year of his gross income into a managed fund. The fees on this fund are 1 per cent per year.

When he takes his pension fund out 50 years later, he pays 20 per cent tax on the fund.

Who has more money – the fund manager or the tax man?

*David Hargreaves, Visiting Lecturer, Faculty of Actuarial Science and Insurance,*
*Cass Business School*

**117** There are only two answers to a quiz question: one is right and one is wrong.

Five steps are required to work out the right answer.

Each time you make a mistake, your answer switches from right to wrong or wrong to right. Each step in the calculation has a 50 per cent chance of being right or wrong.

What is your chance of getting the right answer?

*David Hargreaves, Visiting Lecturer, Faculty of Actuarial Science and Insurance,*
*Cass Business School*

**118**  A standard game of snakes and ladders has 100 squares, eight snakes and eight ladders.

The rules are adapted so that player A rolls two dice and moves by the sum of the two dice. Player B also rolls two dice but then chooses which of the two dice he moves by.

Who is the favourite to win? You may assume player A goes first.

*David Hargreaves, Visiting Lecturer, Faculty of Actuarial Science and Insurance, Cass Business School*

**119**  I put a large rectangular sheet of paper on a table. I then place 100 coins, each of 2cm diameter, flat on the paper without overlapping each other or the table.

Would it be possible for me to place 400 coins each of 1cm diameter in the same way on a sheet of paper identical to the one I have?

*Dr Lynda White, Department of Mathematics, Imperial College London*

**120**  Eleven goblins stand different distances apart at points in a flat field. Each is armed with a water pistol. At the command, each of them fires their water pistol at the goblin nearest to them.

Whatever their initial positions, one of the goblins stays dry. Why?

*Dr Lynda White, Department of Mathematics, Imperial College London*

**121** Seven people sit round a circular table at a Chinese restaurant. They each order a different dish. Unfortunately it's the waiter's first day on the job and he places the wrong dish in front of each of the seven diners. However, as this is a Chinese restaurant, the table can be rotated.

Is it possible to rotate the table so that at least two diners get the dish they ordered?

*Dr Lynda White, Department of Mathematics, Imperial College London*

**122** Joe the milkman has a 4 × 6 rectangular crate that can hold 24 milk bottles, with each cavity capable of holding a single bottle. However, Joe only has 18 bottles.

How many ways can he put these in the crate so that each row and each column has an even number of bottles?

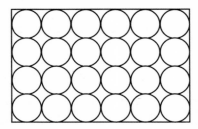

*Dr Lynda White, Department of Mathematics, Imperial College London*

**123** A maths professor of my acquaintance has noticed that the long number N on her credit card has ten digits.

The first digit of N is the number of 0s in N, the second digit is the number of 1s, the third digit is the number of 2s, and so on until the last digit is the number of 9s in N.

What is her credit card number?

*Dr Lynda White, Department of Mathematics, Imperial College London*

**124** Mo Faster just misses his train. Shortly afterwards, another train arrives on the same platform and he boards it. He arrives at his destination sooner than some passengers from the first train.

How did he do it?

*Dr Lynda White, Department of Mathematics, Imperial College London*

**125** Draw six points on a piece of paper and connect each pair of points with either a blue or red line. When all the pairs of points are connected, you'll see that at least one triangle has been formed from all blue or all red lines.

Can you show that this will always happen?

*Dr Steve Humble MBE, Head of Education, Newcastle University*

**126** Is it worth keeping your old calendar? How many years would you have to wait before the same dates fall on exactly the same days of the week so you could use it again?

*Dr Steve Humble MBE, Head of Education, Newcastle University*

**127** If you had two different colours and painted each face of a cube one of these two colours, how many different ways could you paint the cube?

*Dr Steve Humble MBE, Head of Education, Newcastle University*

**128** Using four 4s and any of the operation buttons (e.g. +, -, x, ÷, !, √ ) on a calculator, make the integers from 1 to 20.

For example, one way to form 1 is (4 ÷ 4) + 4 − 4.

*Dr Steve Humble MBE, Head of Education, Newcastle University*

## 129 SIX GLASSES

There are six glasses in a row. From left to right, the first three are filled with water and the other three are empty.

By moving one glass only, can you arrange the glasses so they alternate full and empty?

*Dr Steve Humble MBE, Head of Education, Newcastle University*

## 130 HUSBAND AND WIFE

A husband and wife have a combined age of 77. The husband is now twice as old as his wife was when he was as old as she is now.

How old are the husband and wife?

*Dr Steve Humble MBE, Head of Education, Newcastle University*

## 131 BABY WEIGHTS

The combined weight of a baby boy and baby girl is 7kg. If the baby girl weighs three quarters of the baby boy, how much do both babies weigh?

*Dr Steve Humble MBE, Head of Education, Newcastle University*

## 132 SPINNING COIN

Place a 2p coin on a table. How can you make the coin spin without touching it?

*Dr Steve Humble MBE, Head of Education, Newcastle University*

## 133 SONS' AGES

In a family there are three sons. The eldest is six years older than the second son, who is six years older than the youngest. The youngest is half the age of the eldest.

How old is each son?

*Dr Steve Humble MBE, Head of Education, Newcastle University*

## 134 UPSIDE-DOWN GLASS

Place a piece of cardboard over a glass of water and turn it upside down on a table. Now carefully pull out the cardboard. This leaves the glass upside down on the table with the water still inside.

How can you get the glass the right way up again without spilling water all over the table?

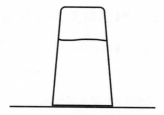

*Dr Steve Humble MBE, Head of Education, Newcastle University*

## 135 SPEND, SPEND, SPEND

You spend one-third of the money in your wallet. Then you spend one-third of what remains.

If you have spent in total £75, how much did you originally have in your wallet?

*Dr Steve Humble MBE, Head of Education, Newcastle University*

**136** A shop owner has £1,000 to spend on pens that cost £7 each and notebooks that cost £13 each.

If the shop owner wants to spend the full £1,000 buying more pens than notebooks, how many alternatives does she have?

*Dr Steve Humble MBE, Head of Education, Newcastle University*

## 137 NOT REALLY A PUZZLE, MORE A CURIOSITY

Read the three questions below and write down the first thing you think of in each case.

First, write down the name of a colour. Most people would write 'red', so don't choose this colour.

........................................................................................

Second, draw a simple geometrical figure, such as a circle or a square.

........................................................................................

Finally, write down a two-digit number between 1 and 50, in which both digits are odd (such as 15). They should not repeat, such as 1 and 1.

........................................................................................

Look in the answers and see if we've correctly predicted your responses.

*Dr Steve Humble MBE, Head of Education, Newcastle University*

## 138 ORANGE AND WATER

I fill a glass half full of orange juice and another glass, twice the size, one-fifth full of orange juice. Then I top up both glasses with water and pour the contents of both into a jug.

How much of the mixture in the jug is water and how much orange juice?

*Dr Steve Humble MBE, Head of Education, Newcastle University*

## 139 TOM, DICK AND HARRY

Tom, Dick and Harry have £500 to share out between them. They agree that Tom will get £10 more than Dick, and Dick will get £20 more than Harry.

How much do they each receive?

*Dr Steve Humble MBE, Head of Education, Newcastle University*

## 140 The total number of spots on three spotty dogs is 98. Grumpy spotty dog has twice as many spots as Sneezy spotty dog, and Happy spotty dog has twice as man spots at Grumpy.

How many spots are there on each of the spotty dogs?

*Dr Steve Humble MBE, Head of Education, Newcastle University*

**141** Peter is older than Tim. The difference between their ages is one-third of the total of their ages.

If on his last birthday Tim was ten years younger than Peter, how old are Peter and Tim?

*Dr Steve Humble MBE, Head of Education, Newcastle University*

**142** A group goes out for lunch at a café. The bill comes to £171. Each man in the group pays £6 and each woman pays £5 towards the bill.

How many different possible groups of men and women could have had lunch at the café?

*Dr Steve Humble MBE, Head of Education, Newcastle University*

**143** In the spirit of reconciliation, four Leavers and four Remainers sit down to lunch at a round table. The seating plan is determined entirely by lot. They say two's company, three or more is an echo chamber. So what's the probability that there will be no echo chambers at the table?

*Yin-Fung Au read Mathematics at Oxford University, and currently teaches the subject at a school in London*

**144** I'm trying to decide which of this season's BBC Proms concerts to attend. As usual, the season spans 75 days, so to help me choose I have 75 pieces of card in front of me, numbered 1 to 75, laid out in order.

Starting with card 1, if the number of pieces of card on the table is divisible by the number on the card, I put it down and move on to the next card in the sequence; otherwise, I tear the card in half before moving on. I stop the process after card 75.

The cards that remain intact tell me which Proms I will attend. Which are those Proms?

*Yin-Fung Au read Mathematics at Oxford University, and currently teaches the subject at a school in London*

**145** The weather is scorching, so I'm packing the most refreshing things I can think of for a picnic.

Cucumber contains 95 per cent water, while melon contains 90 per cent water. After they've been left in the sun all afternoon, however, the cucumber contains 92 per cent water and the melon 85 per cent water.

Which of my picnic items has lost a greater percentage of its mass?

*Yin-Fung Au read Mathematics at Oxford University, and currently teaches the subject at a school in London*

**146** Medical researchers are investigating the use of a new ultra-sensitive breathalyser.

Imagine you could tag all molecules exhaled in Julius Caesar's last breath.

How many of these molecules would a breathalyser be exposed to with one of Caesar's exhalations if you ignore chemical reactions and exchanges, and the fact that the atmosphere is well-mixed?

*Dr Shaun Fitzgerald, Director of the Royal Institution*

**147** With all the ball sports of the summer and a certain frenzy in the air, we have made a solid ball of radius 1m and cut it up into eight equal pieces.

What is the lowest ratio of the surface area to the volume for each of the eight pieces?

*Dr Shaun Fitzgerald, Director of the Royal Institution*

**148** Life expectancy of men is about 79 years and that of women is about 83 years. These should be increasing by two months per year, but this has stopped.

If we can start increasing life expectancy by two months per year again, what is the life expectancy of someone born today?

*Dr Shaun Fitzgerald, Director of the Royal Institution*

**149** In October 2018, the BBC news included a report from the IPCC which stated that the difference between a 1.5 degrees Celsius and a 2 degrees Celsius rise in temperature would cause a further 0.1m rise in sea level.

How much water does this represent in terms we can visualise? If all this water was to cover England, what height would the flood be?

*Dr Shaun Fitzgerald, Director of the Royal Institution*

**150** Cyprus has a fertility rate of 1 child per woman. The average Cypriot has a life expectancy of 80 years, and the population is currently evenly distributed in terms of age and gender.

How long will it take for the population of Cyprus to decrease by 10 per cent with no migration?

*Dr Shaun Fitzgerald, Director of the Royal Institution*

**151** If the value of a bitcoin bounces around between $10,000 and $5,000, varying from high to low each month, and you invest $10,000 each month, what is the average price of each bitcoin you buy?

*Dr Shaun Fitzgerald, Director of the Royal Institution*

**152** A science news story in 2018 was that on an island in the South Atlantic, mice are threatening seabird colonies with extinction. The BBC report says that as a result of their success, the mice have become 'super-sized' and are about 50 per cent larger than a domestic mouse.

Being bigger also helps reduce the surface area to volume ratio that can help animals keep warm.

Assuming a domestic mouse is roughly spherical, what is the reduction in surface area to volume ratio as a result of being 50 per cent bigger?

*Dr Shaun Fitzgerald, Director of the Royal Institution*

**153** An ant is at one corner inside a closed cardboard box.

The box is made up of square faces, 1 metre along each edge.

What is the minimum distance the ant must travel to reach the corner of the box furthest away from their current position?

*School of Mathematics and Statistics at the University of Sheffield*

**154** I have a cube and a tetrahedron in front of me. If I dismantle the cube and lay flat on a table the three squares that meet at a vertex, I find that I'm 'missing' 90°. I call this the 'deficit'. The total deficit for all eight vertices of the cube is therefore 720°.

For the tetrahedron, with three triangles meeting at each of the four vertices, the total deficit is again 720°.

What is the deficit for the other three 'perfect' platonic solids (octahedron, dodecahedron and icosahedron)?

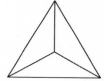 

*Hugh Hunt, Reader in Engineering Dynamics and Vibration at Trinity College, Cambridge*

**155** A 2018 BBC news headline stated that 'The average price of student accommodation in the UK has JUMPED by nearly a third in six years'.

Has it really jumped? What is the actual average annual price increase which this figure corresponds to?

*Dr Shaun Fitzgerald, Director of the Royal Institution*

**156** Add together the biggest internal angle found in a rhombus, in an isosceles triangle, in a right-angled triangle and in a hexagon.

What are the smallest and largest possible answers?

*Hugh Hunt, Reader in Engineering Dynamics and Vibration at Trinity College, Cambridge*

**157** Form an expression equal to 2 using only the number 8 twice and elementary mathematical operations. No other numbers should appear in your expression.

*School of Mathematics and Statistics at the University of Sheffield*

**158** What is next number in the sequence?

**61**

**52**

**63**

**94**

**46**

**18**

*School of Mathematics and Statistics at the University of Sheffield*

**159** You are in New York, at the intersection of 47th and 7th. You want to walk to the intersection of 59th and 5th.

How many different routes can you take if, at each intersection, you travel in a direction that takes you closer to your destination?

*School of Mathematics and Statistics at the University of Sheffield*

**160** Alex has a chain made of 63 gold links. He removes three non-adjacent links, each from somewhere along the chain, not at the ends, so that now he holds these three individual links and four longer sections of chain that have become separated from each other. He has seven pieces of chain altogether.

Alex visits his friend Blair on each of 63 consecutive days. Blair holds no gold links to begin with. On day 1, Alex hands over to Blair one of the individual links, so Blair has one more link than before and Alex has one fewer.

On subsequent visits, they can exchange any number of the seven pieces of chain, but they have to do it in such a way that each day the total number of links held by Blair goes up by one and the number held by Alex goes down by one.

Is there a way for Alex to choose which three links to remove at the beginning, in order that this will be possible?

*School of Mathematics and Statistics at the University of Sheffield*

# CHAPTER 5

---

# ORANGES

---

# AND LEMONS

---

Food and drink have featured prominently in this year's puzzles. Perhaps it's something to do with tackling them over the breakfast table.

There are chocolates, pancakes, ice creams and cocktails to work your way through here — a selection from the smorgasbord that is the #PuzzleForToday.

**161** Two mums enjoy a sunny day out with four kids: Athena, Bill, Cathy and Drew.

The children ask for ice-cream. One of the mums nips across to the café to buy the ice-creams, but she forgets to ask which flavours they want. She decides to buy four different flavours to try to keep each child happy: chocolate, vanilla, strawberry and mango.

When she returns, Bill cheekily swoops past and grabs the mango ice cream. Drew only likes fruit flavours, but Athena really doesn't. And Cathy doesn't like vanilla.

Is there a way of sharing out the ice-creams so that all the children are happy?

*Dr Nicos Georgiou, Senior Lecturer in Mathematics at the University of Sussex*

**162** The Easter Bunny is wrapping chocolate eggs using two wrapping foils of different colours for each egg.

Bunny has 20 red wrapping foils, 8 green ones and 14 yellow ones.

After he has finished, Bunny has a green and a red wrapper left.

How many eggs were wrapped in green and yellow?

*Dr Nicos Georgiou, Senior Lecturer in Mathematics at the University of Sussex*

**163** Andy invited five close friends round for dinner to celebrate his birthday: Ben, Catherine, Danny, Ellen and Fiona. The group of friends had a huge fight earlier that day, but they agree that they will all still attend the dinner party, as long as Andy ensures that:

**1** Andy does not sit next to Fiona, Ellen or Ben

**2** Fiona and Ellen don't sit next to each other

**3** Ben doesn't sit next to Catherine or Danny

**4** Ellen and Catherine don't sit next to each other

Can Andy arrange everybody happily around a circular table?

*Dr Nicos Georgiou, Senior Lecturer in Mathematics at the University of Sussex*

**164** It is Shrove Tuesday and John and Martha are tossing pancakes. John can flip a pancake up to two times in the air whereas Martha can manage three.

What is the probability that they both manage to turn their pancakes over? Assume that they don't drop their pancake on the floor or get it stuck to the ceiling, and that at least one flip is always made.

*Dr Shaun Fitzgerald, Director of the Royal Institution*

**165** John Humphrys has just poured himself a cup of tea, but forgotten that he is about to start a ten-minute interview. He likes his tea as hot as possible and has to decide whether to pour the cold milk from the fridge in before he starts the interview or afterwards.

What should he do?

*Dr Shaun Fitzgerald, Director of the Royal Institution*

**166** For the Notting Hill Carnival, you visit the Seagull & Hammers Drinks Stall for some beverages.

Three rum cocktails and two carrot juices cost £18.

Two rum cocktails and two carrot juices cost £14.

If you decide to lay off the alcohol and just go for the non-alcoholic option, what is the price of just one carrot juice?

*Bobby Seagull (@bobby_seagull) is a school maths teacher and doctorate student in Mathematics Education at Cambridge University. www.bobbyseagull.com*

**167** Former favourite of Queen Elizabeth I, Sir Walter Raleigh, was executed more than 400 years ago, in 1618. What connection is there between Raleigh and the following three clues?

Clue 1: the child monarch whose death is widely attributed to Richard III

Clue 2: the Italian baroque composer from Venice known as the Red Priest

Clue 3: the eldest author of the Brontë sisters.

*Bobby Seagull (@bobby_seagull) is a school maths teacher and doctorate student in Mathematics Education at Cambridge University. www.bobbyseagull.com*

**168** The *Today* programme presenters all take the same amount of sugar in their morning coffee. John only has a foot-high cone of sugar standing on his desk. He slices out the middle 4 inches of sugar and gives it to Nick. He is left with just enough sugar to make three cups of coffee for Martha, Michal and Justin, but not one for himself.

Does Nick have enough sugar to make his own coffee?

*School of Mathematics and Statistics at the University of Sheffield*

**169** While your partner is away, you take delivery of a full barrel of wine on their behalf.

On the first night, you drink five glasses of wine. Fearing your partner might get angry, you top the barrel up with water.

The following night you are thirsty and you drink six glasses of the diluted wine.

You observe that you are equally tipsy on both nights.

How many glasses of wine does the barrel hold?

*School of Mathematics and Statistics at the University of Sheffield*

**170** You have been given a recommendation for the best coffee shop in town. You know the name of the road but not the building number. However, you do recall that the sum of the numbers that divide into the building number is unlucky.

What number building should you visit?

*School of Mathematics and Statistics at the University of Sheffield*

## 171 DOWN IN ONE

John, Justin and Sarah all prepare for the radio show by downing a litre of coffee. They decide to have a race to see who can drink the fastest, when each is drinking at their own uniform speed.

When Sarah finishes, Justin has 100ml left, and when Justin finishes John still has 100ml to go.

How much coffee did John have left when Sarah finished?

*School of Mathematics and Statistics at the University of Sheffield*

**172** There are three boxes. One contains only apples, one contains only oranges and one contains both apples and oranges.

The boxes have been incorrectly labelled, so that no label identifies the correct contents of the box it is on.

You open one box and, without looking inside, take out one piece of fruit.

By looking at the fruit, how can you immediately label all the boxes correctly?

*Dr Elon Correa Lecturer in Mathematics and Statistics, University of Salford*

**173** Eight people go for dinner at a restaurant. Each person is friends with precisely two other people at that party, but no three people know each other.

Is there a way to sit at a round table so that nobody sits next to a person they know?

*Dr Nicos Georgiou, Senior Lecturer in Mathematics at the University of Sussex*

## 174 THE PRICE OF FISH

Fred is looking after his father's fishmonger stall, which sells three types of fish – salmon, cod and tuna. The price list has gone missing but Fred knows that on each of the last three days the stall sold £150 worth of fish.

On Monday the stall sold 10 portions of salmon, 12 of cod and 10 of tuna.

On Tuesday it sold 6 portions of salmon, 15 of cod and 9 of tuna.

On Wednesday it sold 23 portions of salmon, 4 of cod and 12 of tuna.

What price should Fred charge for each portion of fish?

*Sally Calder, Education Actuary, Institute and Faculty of Actuaries*

## 175 A CLASSIC

A bar of chocolate contains three rows of eight squares. How many breaks are needed to separate the bar into 24 squares of chocolate?

*School of Mathematics and Statistics at the University of Sheffield*

## 176 I have two haggis in the fridge.

One weighs twice as much as the other. In cooking them, I know that the time taken to reach the same centre temperature goes as the square of the diameter.

Both haggis are plunged into boiling water and left boiling. The smaller one is ready after one hour, at which point I start playing my bagpipes. I stop playing when the second one is done.

How long does my long long-suffering family have to endure the bagpipes?

*Hugh Hunt, Reader in Engineering Dynamics and Vibration at Trinity College, Cambridge*

## 177 LOYALTY SCHEME

Darren owns a grocery store. He's been running a loyalty card scheme for his customers for several years. The scheme has three tiers:

**BLUE** = basic customer tier

**SILVER** = super customer tier

**GOLD** = super-dooper customer tier

Customers earn loyalty points each time they spend money in the store. The number of points earned over the year determines which tier the customer is in next year.

Customers earning fewer than 1,000 points automatically revert to the BLUE tier (or stay in BLUE if they were already there).

Customers earning 1,000 points or more will move up one tier (or stay in GOLD if they were already there).

One in five customers in each tier earns less than 1,000 points in any one year, with the rest earning more.

At the end of the year, Darren must print off new loyalty cards for next year. However, his computer has crashed and he's lost his records! All he can remember is the total number of customers in the loyalty scheme, which is 2,000.

Assuming the proportion of customers in each tier has been the same for the past few years, can you help Darren work out how many cards of each colour he needs?

*Sally Calder, Education Actuary, Institute and Faculty of Actuaries*

# CHAPTER 6

# POLAR

# PARADOXES

Getting Martha Kearney and the *Today* programme production team to the Natural Environment Research Station at Ny-Alesund on Svalbard was one of the highlights of 2019. Initially, we hoped to mark the occasion with a single polar puzzle.

Instead, we were delighted to discover many ardent puzzlers hiding amongst the climate scientists and microbiologists. Who knew that the team from Manchester and Cambridge, who were in the Arctic to practice their techniques for hunting meteorites 'lost' in the snow and ice ahead of an expedition to Antarctica, would turn up so many puzzling gems?

## 178 WINTER SOLSTICE

On the winter solstice, the North Pole is inclined away from the sun by 23.5°, and it is this tilt that gives us shorter days in winter.

Given that the Arctic Circle is defined as the lowest latitude at which the sun does not rise above the horizon on the winter solstice, at what latitude does the Arctic Circle reside?

*Dr Geoff Evatt, School of Mathematics, University of Manchester*

## 179 AN ARCTIC FOX, A ROCK PTARMIGAN AND SOME POLAR WILLOW

An Arctic biologist needs to move an Arctic fox, a young rock ptarmigan (a kind of grouse) and some polar willow samples from her field site back to the main base using her skidoo trailer.

Left alone, the Arctic fox will attack the rock ptarmigan, and the rock ptarmigan will eat the polar willow.

Only a single specimen can be transported at a time.

How many trips back and forth does it take her to transport all three specimens, and in what order should she take them?

*Dr Andrew Smedley, School of Mathematics, University of Manchester*

## 180 POLAR PARCEL POST

Suvi and her 16-year-old son Thule decide to travel from the North Pole to the South Pole and back again, to raise awareness of the difficulties penguins face in sending presents to their polar bear friends.

They maintain a speed of 8.5 miles per day, and travel for an exact number of years.

Once back at the North Pole (with presents for the polar bears), Thule realises that he is now exactly half of his mother's age (in years), whereas when they set off Suvi was two and a half times the age of Thule.

Use this information to work out the circumference of the Earth around the poles in miles.

*Professor Dave Abrahams, Scientific Director of Isaac Newton Institute for Mathematical Sciences, University of Cambridge*

103

## 181 POLAR BEAR CROSSING

A chilly BBC presenter stands on one side of a 100-m wide fjord in Svalbard. Directly opposite sits a polar bear. Knowing that a polar bear can swim at 10km/h, and the water surface current is flowing at 8km/h, what is the quickest time in which the polar bear can reach the presenter?

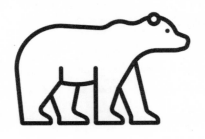

*Dr Geoff Evatt, School of Mathematics, University of Manchester*

## 182 ARCTIC SEA ICE

Since 1979, Arctic sea ice has been declining in mass by some 1.7 per cent per year. Over this period (just half a human lifetime), what proportion of the original sea-ice mass has been lost from the Arctic?

*Dr Geoff Evatt, School of Mathematics, University of Manchester*

# 183 DRILLING FOR ICE

Geoff is undertaking an experiment to detect iron meteorites hidden in the polar ice. He wants to place trial meteorites at precise depths of 10cm, 20cm, 30cm, etc., up to 100cm, but he only has two drill bits of lengths 30cm and 50cm, which have to be inserted fully each time. Geoff can use either or both of these several times in each hole to make a deeper hole.

He also has a measuring jug that can be used to pour water into the hole, which rapidly freezes, thereby reducing the depth of the hole by 40cm.

How can Geoff use the drill bits and the jug to most efficiently plant ten trial meteorites at their required depths?

*Professor Dave Abrahams, Scientific Director of Isaac Newton Institute for*
*Mathematical Sciences, University of Cambridge*

# CHAPTER 7

---
# A QUESTION
---
## OF SPORT
---

Football and cycling seemed to dominate 2019. Perhaps that should come as no surprise after the summer's World Cup and Tour de France.

Still there is always some rugby league, darts and chess for the purists, and some roller-skating and robot Lego for those who prefer their sport more esoteric. Sadly Garry's racing tips failed to reach the starting line this year.

**184** What connects Champions League teams

Real Madrid in 1958,

Ajax in 1973,

Bayern Munich in 1976

and Real Madrid again in 2018?

*Bobby Seagull (@bobby_seagull) is a school maths teacher and doctorate student in Mathematics Education at Cambridge University. www.bobbyseagull.com*

**185** The Grand Final of Rugby League's 2018 Super League saw Wigan Warriors defeat Warrington Wolves 12–4. For the following puzzle, answer what immediately comes to mind!

During half-time at the final, you buy a souvenir t-shirt and a bottle of water. Together they cost £11. The souvenir t-shirt costs £10 more than the bottle of water.

How much does the bottle of water cost?

*Bobby Seagull (@bobby_seagull) is a school maths teacher and doctorate student in Mathematics Education at Cambridge University. www.bobbyseagull.com*

**186** To celebrate the 29th Annual Left Handers Day, four prominent left-handed people gathered together: Barack Obama, Bill Gates, Sir Paul McCartney and Paula Radcliffe. They were asked to strategically select four football clubs to visit on this day to honour left-handedness.

Obama selected West Ham

Gates selected Manchester City

McCartney selected Portsmouth

and Radcliffe selected Burnley.

Why was this?

*Bobby Seagull (@bobby_seagull) is a school maths teacher and doctorate student in Mathematics Education at Cambridge University. www.bobbyseagull.com*

**187** *Strictly Come Dancing* judges Craig, Darcey, Shirley and Bruno each give the finalists a score between 1 and 10 for their performance. One dancer does an unusual Christmas dance in the style of a reindeer, attracting a disagreement in scores from the judges.

Bruno and Shirley both give a score that is double Craig's score.

If the average score for this dancer is 6 and Darcey gives a score of 9, what scores were awarded by Bruno, Shirley and Craig?

*Bobby Seagull (@bobby_seagull) is a school maths teacher and doctorate student in Mathematics Education at Cambridge University. www.bobbyseagull.com*

**188** Riders in the Tour de France can reach astonishing speeds, but it's slow going up the mountains. During one stage – a distance of 120km – Geraint Thomas maintained a speed of 60km/h over the first 60km and 20km/h over the remaining distance – the uphill stretch.

What was his average speed?

(By the way, the answer isn't 40km/h)!

*Hugh Hunt, Reader in Engineering Dynamics and Vibration at Trinity College, Cambridge*

**189** Chris Froome was riding his bike on Stage 11 of the Tour de France when he cycled over a small patch of wet paint. This left a bright yellow spot on his front tyre.

If Chris is riding at a steady speed of 40km/h, what is the maximum speed of the spot?

*Hugh Hunt, Reader in Engineering Dynamics and Vibration at Trinity College, Cambridge*

## 190 PERFECT PENALTIES

All England players acquire the ability to miss or score a penalty at will. England meets Germany, and the game goes to penalties with Germany going first.

Knowing that they will win, the England players decide to bring the game to sudden death, for added drama, by choosing to score whenever Germany scores and to miss whenever Germany misses.

In how many possible ways can the game progress to sudden death?

*School of Mathematics and Statistics at the University of Sheffield*

**191** A father and son have enjoyed roller skating together for the last few weeks. The father is quite a bit larger and heavier than the boy.

The family are heading to Northern Europe for a winter holiday, and the father and son are keen to have a go at ice skating. They purchase ice skates with the same blades. When they set off to skate, the father moves off gracefully but his son can't move.

Why not?

*Dr Shaun Fitzgerald, Director of the Royal Institution*

**192** What is the largest number of bishops that you can put on a chess board so that no two are attacking each another?

*School of Mathematics and Statistics at the University of Sheffield*

**193** With three scoring darts on a conventional dartboard, the lowest possible score is 3 and the highest score is 180. There are some impossible scores like 179.

What is the lowest impossible score between 3 and 180?

*Hugh Hunt, Reader in Engineering Dynamics and Vibration at Trinity College, Cambridge*

**194** There are 32 white squares on a chess board. Your task is to draw a line once only through all the white squares, moving via the corners where they touch without entering any of the black squares and without lifting your pen off the board.

Can this be done? If not, how many separate lines are required?

*Hugh Hunt, Reader in Engineering Dynamics and Vibration at Trinity College, Cambridge*

## 195 BALLS AND RED FACES

A classic football is made from 20 white hexagons and 12 black pentagons. Whichever of the 20 white hexagons I choose to paint red, the outcome looks the same, because I can rotate the ball.

How many different-looking footballs can I create by choosing a second white hexagon to paint red?

*School of Mathematics and Statistics at the University of Sheffield*

**196** Inspired by the Tour de France, a child decides to investigate her bicycle.

A parent holds the bike to prevent it from falling over while the child arranges the pedals to be vertically positioned – i.e. one at the top, one at the bottom.

The child is standing on the floor and pushes the bottom pedal backwards.

Which way does the bicycle move?

*Dr Shaun Fitzgerald, Director of the Royal Institution*

## 197 BICYCLE SHOP

Bob runs a bicycle shop. He stocks 40 different models of bicycle, all of which are equally popular with cyclists.

He expects to sell 20 bicycles next month.

What is the chance that he'll sell at least two identical bicycles?

*Sally Calder, Education Actuary, Institute and Faculty of Actuaries*

**198** In the women's football world cup, 51 games take place to find the winner from 24 teams. What is the fewest number of games that could be used to find the winner from 24 teams?

*Kyle D Evans (@kyledevans) is an award-winning maths communicator and Head of Maths at Barton Peveril College. www.kyledevans.com*

**199** How many different sequences of opponents could England encounter on a successful route to the World Cup final, including the final itself?

*School of Mathematics and Statistics at the University of Sheffield*

**200** There are 20 teams in the Premier League, and in a season each team plays all the others home and away.

How many matches are played in total in the entire division over the course of one season?

*Bobby Seagull (@bobby_seagull) is a school maths teacher and doctorate student in Mathematics Education at Cambridge University. www.bobbyseagull.com*

**201** A one-armed boxer only knows how to throw a jab and an uppercut. They do not have the ability to throw consecutive uppercuts.

How many different seven-punch combos can they do?

*School of Mathematics and Statistics at the University of Sheffield*

**202** In the final of the 2015 women's world cup, USA beat Japan 5–2. In how many possible orders could the goals in that game have been scored?

*Kyle D Evans (@kyledevans) is an award-winning maths communicator and Head of Maths at Barton Peveril College. www.kyledevans.com*

# CHAPTER 8

---

# PRESENTER

---

# PROBLEMS

---

Martha Kearney makes her debut in the #PuzzleForToday this year and it's good to see she's holding her end up when it comes to coin tossing with John and racing Nick to Brighton.

I've no idea who the new *Today* programme assistant is, but he'll do fine once he realises the presenters should get their own coffee.

**203** Nick Robinson keeps tossing a fair coin and records the outcome of each toss.

John Humphrys bets five pounds that if he reads the record of the tosses out loud, the arrangement heads–tails–heads will show up 'very early'.

Mishal Husain laughs a bit and says: 'Why don't we make this interesting John? I bet five pounds that heads–heads–tails will show up earlier than your head–tails–heads.

Should John take the bet?

*Dr Nicos Georgiou, Senior Lecturer in Mathematics at the University of Sussex*

**204** Mishal Husain is in a red go-cart and Nick Robinson is in a blue go-cart. They start moving around a circular track from the same spot, but in opposite directions.

The track has a circumference of 60km. Mishal drives at 20km/h and Nick at 30km/h.

How many times do they pass each other on the track before meeting again at the starting point?

*Dr Nicos Georgiou, Senior Lecturer in Mathematics at the University of Sussex*

**205** John Humphrys and Martha Kearney are sitting on a bench in the park, eating their sandwiches and doing a bit of people-watching. They notice two women and a man moving around with their four pets – a snake, a cat and two dogs. The presenters witness an incident between these three people and their pets, which they discuss:

**John:** 'Her snake was scared of the blonde woman with the cat.'

**Martha:** 'Oh, quite! That cat was really aggressive, even that golden retriever started chewing his owner's ponytail from discomfort when he saw her.'

**John:** 'Right… But really, that blue-haired individual did have trouble walking both pets at the same time. It was impossible for him to keep them from fighting.'

They are overheard by a detective novelist, who turns around to get a glimpse of the group John and Martha are talking about. But the novelist only sees the one with the shaved head.

Can she identify from this conversation the hair and pet of each person?

*Dr Nicos Georgiou, Senior Lecturer in Mathematics at the University of Sussex*

**206** Martha Kearney and Nick Robinson are supposed to leave Broadcasting House immediately after the programme ends to catch a train for Brighton.

When they arrive at Victoria Station, Nick manages to buy a ticket first and catches the 10:12 slow train to Brighton, which travels at an average speed of 55km/h.

Unfortunately, he didn't notice that Martha was recognised by a fan and – too polite to avoid the conversation – she missed the train! Instead she caught the 10:24 Gatwick Express, which had an average speed of 70km/h.

If the distance to Brighton is 70km, how far from Brighton will Martha's train be when it overtakes Nick's?

*Dr Nicos Georgiou, Senior Lecturer in Mathematics at the University of Sussex*

**207** The new office assistant at the *Today* programme hasn't got off to a great start. His approach to apostrophes is simply atrocious: he is liable to put one in any word with at least three letters ending with an 's'. Even worse, he never gets two places for apostrophes right in a row.

How many ways could he type this puzzle incorrectly?

*The Maths Department, Oxford High School GDST*

**208** Justin Webb shows Mishal Husain a magic trick.

**Part 1:** He takes 200 balls, each one numbered 1 to 200, and seven boxes. He uses a sneaky way to separate all the balls into the seven boxes and after that he is blindfolded. He then asks Mishal to pick a box at random, pick five random balls from that box, add the numbers on them and give him the total sum. He then correctly tells her from which box she selected the five balls.

How did Justin separate the balls in the first place to allow him to identify the correct box?

**Part 2:** Justin does the trick again. This time, in order to make the trick more difficult, he makes sure that each box contains at least one ball from each group of 1–10, 11–20, 21–30, ... 191–200. He then asks Mishal to again pick a box at random, pick five random balls from that box, add the numbers on them and give him the total sum.

How did he separate the balls so that he can correctly identify the box?

*Dr Nicos Georgiou, Senior Lecturer in Mathematics at the University of Sussex*

**209** Trains between London and Edinburgh take six hours either way. Trains leave London on the hour and they leave Edinburgh on the half hour. They run from 6am to 10pm. Mishal Husain gets on the noon train from London to Edinburgh.

How many trains from Edinburgh to London will her train cross during the journey?

*School of Mathematics and Statistics at the University of Sheffield*

**210** The new office assistant is still causing havoc. He's mixed up the coffee orders for four members of staff every day so far.

Interestingly, he's managed to do this in a different way each day. Tomorrow, though, he will either give someone the right coffee or repeat one of the wrong patterns.

How many days has he worked there?

*The Maths Department, Oxford High School GDST*

**211** In an attempt to apologise for the coffee fiasco, the new office assistant has prepared Martha Kearney's morning bagel in an unusual way. Unfortunately, he didn't realise that Martha usually shares her bagel with Justin Webb. Although the assistant has cut the bagel into two distinct equal pieces, Martha is unable to give Justin one of them.

How was the bagel cut?

*The Maths Department, Oxford High School GDST*

**212** On a recent trip to the National Museum of Computing, the *Today* team got to type their names on to old-fashioned computer tape, where each letter is recorded as a row of holes corresponding to its binary representation – A as 1, B as 2, C as 3 and ignoring the case of the letter.

When they later tried to decode each other's tapes, they quickly realised that they must have got the wrong end of the stick. 'Mishal' came out as V-R-Y-B-P-F and 'Justin' as J-U-Y-E-R-N, while John couldn't figure out what the second letter of his name was.

The new assistant was surprised to see that his name was largely correct, with only the fourth and fifth letters of his six-letter name having changed.

What is the new assistant called?

*The Maths Department, Oxford High School GDST*

**213** John Humphrys, Mishal Husain and Justin Webb are having a debate.

Justin says that both John and Mishal are wrong.

John says that Mishal is wrong.

Mishal says that Justin is right.

Which of the three presenters is right?

*School of Mathematics and Statistics at the University of Sheffield*

**214** John Humphrys, Martha Kearney and Justin Webb are having an interview duel. Each presenter in turn gets to ask one of the others a tough question with the aim of reducing them to a gibbering wreck.

John has a 100 per cent success rate.

Martha manages this two-thirds of the time.

Only 1 in 3 of Justin's questions has this effect.

To mitigate this, the questioning order is Justin, Martha, John.

What is Justin's best strategy?

*The Maths Department, Oxford High School GDST*

**215** With only a few minutes to get the studio ready before the next broadcast, the new assistant is in despair over the state of the headphone cords. Three of them are hanging down and braided together, each one crossing over or under its immediate neighbour.

In his rush, the assistant unplugs all three cords and spends too long untangling them, making Thought for the Day late to air.

John points out to him that he only needed to unplug one of the cords and then the other two would have been easy to separate. It didn't matter which of the three was unplugged for this to happen.

What was the minimum number of crossings in the braid?

*The Maths Department, Oxford High School GDST*

**216** The day after John Humphrys's retirement, Nick buys cake to share with Justin, Mishal and Martha. At lunchtime he finds the cake has been eaten! Nick knows that at least one of the other presenters ate the cake and that they never lie.

**Justin:** 'If Martha ate the cake then so did Mishal.'

**Martha:** 'I know that Mishal would not eat the cake unless Justin ate some.'

**Mishal:** 'Martha eats cake whenever Justin does.'

Who ate all the cake?

*Prathan Jarupoonphol, Ph.D. candidate in mathematics at the University of Sheffield*

## 217 SQUASH SHOTS

John Humphrys and Justin Webb play a game of squash. The ball comes to John, who is exactly 1m from the front wall. He notices that Justin is clinging exhaustedly to the side wall, 3m from the front. John generously plays the ball so that it goes to Justin.

If it travels 5m on its way, how far apart were they standing when it was played?

*School of Mathematics and Statistics at the University of Sheffield*

**218** John Humphrys and Mishal Husain buy a box of 500 chocolates to share between them. The chocolates are labelled 1, 2, 3, 4, 5, and so on up to 500.

John is allowed to eat all the chocolates labelled following the arithmetic sequence 5, 10, 15, 20 ….

Mishal is allowed to eat all the chocolates labelled following the arithmetic sequence 7, 14, 21, 28 ….

If they are both allowed to eat the same chocolate, they decide that to be fair, neither of them should eat it.

How many chocolates will be left uneaten?

*Mr Ryan Glass, Teacher of Mathematics at Sevenoaks School*

**219** Martha Kearney and John Humphrys go off for a 15-mile bike ride. They ride at 10mph.

After 10 miles, John gets a puncture and has to walk his bike the rest of the way. Martha doesn't notice John's predicament and rides on ahead.

When John finally arrives, Martha remarks that she'd been waiting the same length of time as she'd been riding.

What is John's walking speed?

*Hugh Hunt, Reader in Engineering Dynamics and Vibration at Trinity College, Cambridge*

**220** John Humphrys is making raspberry jam from this year's bumper harvest of raspberries. He fills a number of jars with jam, but one jar is only half full. He evens this out by scooping jam from the full jars into the half-full jar so that they are all 90 per cent full.

How many jars of jam has John made?

*Hugh Hunt, Reader in Engineering Dynamics and Vibration at Trinity College, Cambridge*

**221** John Humphrys is reading out the time at about quarter to nine and gets it all wrong (which is not at all unusual). Martha Kearney comes to the rescue, explaining: 'The reason that you're confused, John, is because the hour hand is hidden directly behind the minute hand.'

What is the time?

*Hugh Hunt, Reader in Engineering Dynamics and Vibration at Trinity College, Cambridge*

**222** John Humphrys and Martha Kearney find an old box with two lengths of rope inside, marked '40-minute fuse'.

If one of these ropes is lit with a match from either end, it will take 40 minutes for the rope to burn completely. If they wanted to time 20 minutes, then they could light both ends of one rope simultaneously.

Suppose John and Martha want to time 30 minutes. How do they do it without cutting or measuring the ropes?

*Hugh Hunt, Reader in Engineering Dynamics and Vibration at Trinity College, Cambridge*

**223** For John Humphrys' birthday, Martha Kearney wrapped a present. It was a simple box and she used a single colour of paper on each of the six sides.

How many colours of paper did Martha need to be sure that no adjacent face shared the same colour?

*Hugh Hunt, Reader in Engineering Dynamics and Vibration at Trinity College, Cambridge*

**224** John Humphrys and Martha Kearney are measuring the girth of huge trees in an ancient forest.

John has his tape measure around one tree, recording a circumference of 628cm.

Martha is standing 1m away from the tree.

How much of the tape can Martha see?

*Hugh Hunt, Reader in Engineering Dynamics and Vibration at Trinity College, Cambridge*

**225** It's the end of the summer and John Humphrys has bought a perfectly-spherical watermelon. He carves a large cylindrical hole symmetrically right through the melon. The length of the hole is 20cm. He asks Martha Kearney to work out the volume of the remaining melon.

'Don't I need to know the diameter of the hole?' Martha asks.

'No you don't,' replies John.

What is the volume of the remaining melon?

*Hugh Hunt, Reader in Engineering Dynamics and Vibration at Trinity College, Cambridge*

**226** Sarah Montague has £200 to buy John Humphrys a leaving present.

John likes toffees, trees and money but not quiz books.

Mishal Husain, Justin Webb, Nick Robinson and Martha Kearney like a laugh.

A bag of quality toffees cost £10 and a small tree costs £35.

If Sarah has to spend exactly £200 buying some combination of toffees and trees for John's leaving present, how many alternatives does she have?

*Dr Steve Humble MBE, Head of Education, Newcastle University*

**227** Martha Kearney is looking at necklaces in a jeweller's shop window, hoping that John Humphrys might buy her one for her birthday. There is a thin chain on display with a heavy pendant. It's on a smooth conical stand and she wonders why the chain doesn't slip off with such a heavy pendant.

What is the minimum cone angle needed to prevent the weight of the pendant from pulling the necklace off the stand?

*Hugh Hunt, Reader in Engineering Dynamics and Vibration at Trinity College, Cambridge*

**228** Today is Martha Kearney's birthday and it's martinis all round after the show. Martini glasses are conical and everyone's glass has been filled to half depth, except Martha's, which is full to the brim.

How much more martini does Martha have than everyone else?

*Hugh Hunt, Reader in Engineering Dynamics and Vibration at Trinity College, Cambridge*

# CHAPTER 9

# CHRISTMAS

# CRACKERS

The countdown to Christmas always seems to inspire our puzzle setters and I'm happy to say this year is no exception. The presenters also make a welcome reappearance in this chapter – and why not, generous gift-giving souls that they are?

Whether you love the traditional 'twelve days of Christmas', a more modern, office-bound 'secret Santa' approach, or the full-on magic of spells and fairy dust… it's all here.

## 229 SECRET SANTA

John Humphrys, Mishal Husain, Justin Webb, Martha Kearney and Nick Robinson are very excited because they are having a *Today* programme Secret Santa. They have brought in Christmas tree ornaments to exchange.

 John brought a bauble,

 Mishal a silver pinecone,

 Justin an angel,

 Martha a gold star

 and Nick brought a little Santa.

Luckily, after the first round of Secret Santa no one ended up with his or her own ornament. John and Justin did not end up with either the pinecone or the star, and Nick got the bauble.

What did Mishal get?

*Dr Nicos Georgiou, Senior Lecturer in Mathematics at the University of Sussex*

**230** How many legs are there in 'The Twelve Days of Christmas'?

*Dr Tom Crawford, University of Oxford/Tom Rocks Maths*

## 231 PRESENTS

Andrew, Bill and Cathy are each getting a present from their parents. They see the presents under the tree – red, blue and green – but they don't know which present is for whom or what the box contains. They do know that one of them will get a Christmas jumper, though, which none of them wants!

The children have been pestering their parents to tell them which present is for whom for hours. Finally, their mother gives up and tells them a few clues so they can figure it out. She says: 'Andrew is getting the blue-wrapped gift, but it is not the robot. Cathy will not get the red-wrapped gift, which contains books.' A moment later Bill starts laughing and says to his mother, 'Okay, now that we know who gets what, can we please open them?'

Which gift is wrapped in each colour, and who gets it?

*Dr Nicos Georgiou, Senior Lecturer in Mathematics at the University of Sussex*

**232** You want to arrange 24 Christmas baubles in a rectangle. How many different rectangles can you create?

*Dr Tom Crawford, University of Oxford/Tom Rocks Maths*

## 233 BABYSITTING DURING CHRISTMAS DINNER

Simon and Ellen are hosting this year's holiday dinner. In order to seat all their guests, they need two different dinner tables – one for the children aged under 18 and one for the adults. They are not sure how many people will come but they definitely expect between 11 and 15 children, so the round children's table has 16 chairs.

They tell their son Will (who is turning 18 on 25 December) that he will have to sit at the children's table to look after the younger kids, at which point he starts laughing and says: 'I'll tell you what, I will do it if no three children can sit next to each other, otherwise it will be impossible to babysit them!' His parents hastily agree, not noticing how smug Will looks!

Is Will going to babysit in the end?

*Dr Nicos Georgiou, Senior Lecturer in Mathematics at the University of Sussex*

**234** John has embraced the Twelve Days of Christmas and is going to send presents to his true love – one on the first day, two on the second day, etc. He goes overboard and thinks about continuing the pattern until next Christmas.

How many presents will he need to find?

*Dr Shaun Fitzgerald, Director of the Royal Institution*

# 235 SANTA'S LITTLE HELPERS

Santa has finished preparing the gifts for everyone who has been nice. He finally starts wrapping the gifts for his little elves, but he realises that he can't quite remember how many elves work in his house! The only thing he remembers is that the number of elves working there is a two-digit number with the same digit (so one of 11, 22, 33, ..., 99).

He asks the youngest elf, Athena, to play a game with him. If she completes the game, she will receive two extra presents. Delighted, Athena agrees.

Santa tells her to do the following operations in order:

**1.** Think of the number of elves who work in my house and multiply it by 100.

**2.** Add 33 to that number.

**3.** Divide the result by 11. This should be a three-digit number.

**4.** Write the number in reverse order and add the two three-digit numbers together.

**5.** Divide the result by 101 and tell me what you got.

Athena starts giggling and says she's got 12.

Santa gives her the two extra presents and starts preparing the remaining presents for all his workers.

How many elves work for Santa?

*Dr Nicos Georgiou, Senior Lecturer in Mathematics at the University of Sussex*

**236** The government wants to host a Christmas firework display that everyone on the UK mainland can enjoy. The government chooses the Isle of Man as the location for the display, which provides a launch place reasonably equidistant from the extremities of the mainland.

Assuming it is a wonderfully clear night, how high does the really bright firework need to be in order to be seen by everyone?

*Dr Shaun Fitzgerald, Director of the Royal Institution*

**237** Christmas stamps are sold with the following values: 16p, 17p, 23p, 24p, 39p and 40p. You want to send a present with a postage cost of £1.

How many stamps do you need to buy to make the exact amount?

*Dr Tom Crawford, University of Oxford/Tom Rocks Maths*

**238** On Christmas night, Santa needs to travel the circumference of the Earth – 24,901 miles – to deliver presents.

He has four sacks of carrots to feed his reindeer. Each sack contains ten carrots to give a total of 40.

He must feed the reindeer one carrot per 1,000 miles travelled, plus an extra one carrot for every sack carried for 5,000 miles.

Does he have enough carrots to complete his journey?

*Dr Tom Crawford, University of Oxford/Tom Rocks Maths*

**239** Santa's workshop has 100 lockers – one for each of the 100 elves who help him make toys for Christmas. The lockers are numbered 1 to 100.

On the first day of work, Santa asks elf number 1 to open all lockers, elf number 2 to close all lockers whose numbers are multiples of 2, elf number 3 to reverse all lockers whose numbers are multiples of 3 (i.e., close it if it is open or open it if it is closed), elf number 4 to do the same to all lockers whose numbers are multiples of 4, and so on. The process is completed with the 100th elf.

How many lockers are open at the end of the process?

| 1 | 2 | 3 | 4 | 5 | 6 | 7 | 8 | 9 | 10 |
|----|----|----|----|----|----|----|----|----|----|
| 11 | 2 | 13 | 14 | 15 | 16 | 17 | 18 | 19 | 20 |
| 21 | 22 | 23 | 24 | 25 | 26 | 27 | 28 | 29 | 30 |
| 31 | 32 | 33 | 34 | 35 | 36 | 37 | 38 | 39 | 40 |
| 41 | 42 | 43 | 44 | 45 | 46 | 47 | 48 | 49 | 50 |
| 51 | 52 | 53 | 54 | 55 | 56 | 57 | 58 | 59 | 60 |
| 61 | 62 | 63 | 64 | 65 | 66 | 67 | 68 | 69 | 70 |
| 71 | 72 | 73 | 74 | 75 | 76 | 77 | 78 | 79 | 80 |
| 81 | 82 | 83 | 84 | 85 | 86 | 87 | 88 | 89 | 90 |
| 91 | 92 | 93 | 94 | 95 | 96 | 97 | 98 | 99 | 100 |

*Dr Elon Correa, Lecturer in Mathematics and Statistics, University of Salford*

**240** The BBC Good Food website tells Santa that he should leave his turkey in the oven for three hours. So, on Christmas Day, he puts the turkey in the oven and, taking a clock with him, he pops out for a ride around the world on his sleigh.

When he returns home, his clock tells him that three hours have passed but when he takes his turkey out of the oven it's completely overdone!

What went wrong?

*Dr Elon Correa, Lecturer in Mathematics and Statistics, University of Salford*

**241** John Humphrys is spending the night in a stable. The three wise *Today* programme presenters Mishal Husain, Martha Kearney and Justin Webb want to present him with the gifts of a cold, fashion sense and a mare.

In how many different ways can the three gifts be divided among the three wise presenters to give to John?

*Dr Elon Correa, Lecturer in Mathematics and Statistics, University of Salford*

**242** You open up a Christmas cracker and instead of a joke, you find a puzzle on a piece of paper.

It reads:

'Complete the following everyday sequence:

Luna,

Mars,

Mercury,

Jupiter,

... And which is the odd one out?'

Can you solve it?

*Bobby Seagull (@bobby_seagull) is a school maths teacher and doctorate student in Mathematics Education at Cambridge University. www.bobbyseagull.com*

**243** I take my sausage-meat stuffing balls out of a 180-degrees Celsius oven and put them on a surface in my 20-degrees Celsius kitchen. Five minutes later, they have only cooled to 100 degrees. To speed things up, I put them outside at freezing point.

How long is it before they are safe to eat at 50 degrees Celsius?

*Dr Elon Correa, Lecturer in Mathematics and Statistics, University of Salford*

**244** You're working on a crossword on Boxing Day, and you notice that you use all of the letters of the alphabet once, except L, which you do not use at all.

Why is this puzzle particularly fitting for the time of year?

*School of Mathematics and Statistics at the University of Sheffield*

**245** A father decides to do some running exercise to get ready for the Christmas season with his young daughter.

Outside their house, there are four trees equally spaced out in a straight line. The distance from each tree to the next tree is 25m.

Before they start running, the father asks his daughter a quick maths question: 'What is the distance between the first tree and the last?'

Can you answer his question?

*Bobby Seagull (@bobby_seagull) is a school maths teacher and doctorate student in Mathematics Education at Cambridge University. www.bobbyseagull.com*

**246** This year we're buying a smaller Christmas tree. It's half the weight of last year's tree.

Last year we needed 12m of tinsel and 24 baubles to decorate the tree tastefully.

Using the same decorations as last year, how much tinsel and how many baubles will we need this year?

*Hugh Hunt, Reader in Engineering Dynamics and Vibration at Trinity College, Cambridge*

**247** My Christmas tree has three sets of lights on it. All three have that annoying box with a button to select the flashing mode. There are eight modes, one for 'steady' and the other seven for 'flashing' in a variety of exciting patterns. When the lights are switched on they start up in one of the eight modes at random.

What is the chance that at least one set of lights is flashing and that I'll be annoyed?

*Hugh Hunt, Reader in Engineering Dynamics and Vibration at Trinity College, Cambridge*

**248** I have some large spherical baubles made of very thin glass. One of them is twice the size of all the others, and it weighs eight times as much.

Is the glass thicker or thinner? By how much?

*Hugh Hunt, Reader in Engineering Dynamics and Vibration at Trinity College, Cambridge*

**249** I'm making mulled wine. Unfortunately I've boiled off all the alcohol so I decide to add some whisky, which is 40 per cent alcohol by volume. The fruit in the boiled mull is also 40 per cent by volume.

How much whisky do I add to 1 litre of my mull to get an end product in which the liquid is 10 per cent alcohol by volume?

*Hugh Hunt, Reader in Engineering Dynamics and Vibration at Trinity College, Cambridge*

**250** We're doing Secret Santa for Christmas in the office. There are four of us. We each buy a gift, wrap it and put it in a sack.

Everyone takes it in turns to pick a gift from the bag. They can tell from the wrapping paper which is their own gift, so they avoid picking that one.

I've volunteered to be Santa, which means I get to hold the sack and I am left with the last remaining package.

What is the probability that I end up with my own gift?

*Hugh Hunt, Reader in Engineering Dynamics and Vibration at Trinity College, Cambridge*

**251** In the Christmas song 'The Twelve Days of Christmas', how many gifts does my true love send to me?

*Hugh Hunt, Reader in Engineering Dynamics and Vibration at Trinity College, Cambridge*

# THE
# ANSWERS

**1**      About 48kg. The volume of the Royal Albert Hall is about 100,000m³
($\pi \times 45 \times 35 \times 20$). Air density is 1.2kg/m³ so there is about 120,000kg
of air in the hall. At 400 parts per million $CO_2$ there is about
$400 \times 120,000/1,000,000 = 48$kg.

**2**      200ml. If you assume that glass is infinitely dense (i.e. occupies zero
volume), then the jar displaces 400ml of water and the upwards buoyancy
force when the jar is on the verge of sinking is 400g. That means that
only 100g of water is needed in addition to the weight of the jar to
make it sink. However, the density of glass is three times that of water, so
the volume of the 300g jar is 100ml and it displaces an extra 100ml of
water. The total buoyancy force on the verge of sinking is therefore 500g,
so 200ml of water is needed to make it sink.

**3**      60. My walking speed on the stationary escalator is shown to be half that
of the escalator speed, so I walk up the moving escalator one and a half
times quicker than I ascend when standing; 40 steps walking is 60 steps
standing.

**4**    The miserly mathematician was thinking of the weight value of each coin:

One 1p coin weighs 3.56g
One 2p coin weighs 7.12g
One 5p coin weighs 3.25g
One 10p coin weighs 6.5g
One 20p coin weighs 5g
One 50p coin weighs 8g

By assigning the weight value to each coin accordingly, five 2p coins are equivalent to ten 1p coins, ten 10p coins are equivalent to twenty 5p coins and five 50p coins are equivalent to eight 20p coins.

**5**    The note from blowing is governed by the air space, which gets smaller, producing a higher note. The note from tapping depends on the wall of the bottle vibrating; adding water increases the moving mass of glass, resulting in a lower note.

**6**    The apple and the balloon stay still; the bag of sand descends. Both apple and balloon are governed by Archimedes' principle: the apple displaces its weight in water and the balloon displaces its weight in air. The elevator accelerating upwards increases the apparent weight of everything, so there is no change. The bag of sand is held up by the rubber band and upwards acceleration requires an additional force (Newton's Law $F = ma$), so the rubber band stretches (Hooke's Law $F = kx$).

**7**    1, 1, 2 and 4. These numbers give both a sum and a product of 8.

**8**    05:50. The other possible answers are 01:10, 02:20, 10:01 and 11:11, but the latter two are too late to require an alarm clock, and the first two are too early even for *Today* presenters to rise!

**9**    132 days. It could happen on the first 12 days of any month, excluding the day where the month number matches the day number, such as 1st January, 6th June, etc.

**10**   The time was 12:34 on 5/6/78 (12345678).

**11**   They are sharing out the letters in the word seven. Each of the five people takes one letter each, so that there are none left over.

**12** The probability is 1 in 60. HAPPY is a five-letter word. If there were no repeating letters, the number of arrangements would be 5! = 120 (Note: ! means factorial, so 5! means 5 × 4 × 3 × 2 × 1). However, since there are repeating letters, you have to divide to remove the duplicates. There are 2 Ps, so 120/2! = 120/2 = 60 ways of arranging the papers.

**13** There are numerous ways to calculate this. One way is to consider that Dennis travelled 5km in that 30-minute head start, so Minnie had to catch up 5km. Her relative speed is 5km/h quicker so it will take her one hour to catch up. That means she caught up at 1.30pm.

**14** 28 people chose ginger beer. 30 per cent = 24 people, so 10 per cent = 8 people and thus 100 per cent = 80 people. Percentage of people who chose ginger beer = 100 − 20 − 15 − 30 = 35 per cent. 35 per cent of 80 = 28.

**15** 2½ hours. 1/5 + 1/3 = 3/15 + 5/15 = 8/15. The remaining time is 7/15 = 70 minutes. So 15/15 = 150 minutes (2 hours 30 minutes).

**16** Superstition. Clue 1: Sit. Clue 2: Eruptions.

**17**    £125. Current price of £100 is 80 per cent. That means 1 per cent is £1.25, so the original price is 100 per cent = £125 (not, as many might think, £120.)

**18**    Yes. The number 40 has this property.

**19**    Five minutes. Your gut might tell you the answer is 100 minutes, but if it takes five robotic builders five minutes to make five hats, then one builder is making one hat in five minutes. That means 100 builders could make 100 hats in the same amount of time.

**20**    The capital cities of the permanent members are London (UK), Washington, D.C. (USA), Moscow (Russia), Beijing (China) and Paris (France). The capitals of the replacement countries each begin with the same letter as one of the original capitals: Lisbon, Wellington, Monrovia, Buenos Aires and Phnom Penh.

**21**    150 degrees. A quarter = 90 degrees. A third = 120 degrees. 90 + 120 = 210.

Total pie is 360 degrees, so 360 − 210 = 150.

**22**  1 in 13,983,816.

$6/49 \times 5/48 \times 4/47 \times 3/46 \times 2/45 \times 1/44 = 720/10,068,347,520 = 1/13,983,816$

**23**  Two years. There are two ways to work this out.

You can write out the number series, which reveals that the first time they all coincide is after two years:

Earth = 0, 1, 2

Mercury = 0, 1/4, 2/4, 3/4, 4/4, 5/4, 6/4, 7/4, 8/4

Venus = 0, 2/3, 4/3, 6/3

Alternatively, you can find the lowest common multiple of 1, 1/4 and 2/3, which is two.

**24**  Six. Student A high-fives with students B, C and D. Then student B high-fives with students C and D. Then student C high-fives student D. $3 + 2 + 1 = 6$.

**25**    Pig sweets = £2 each. Dog sweets = 50p each.

You can set up simultaneous equations or solve by inspection. Peter buys two pig sweets more for an additional £4. So pig sweets are £2 each. This means that two dog sweets cost £1, so one costs half that – 50p.

**26**    A joey is missing.

Prophetic Greek deity = Phoebe

German steed = (das) Ross

Jewish matriarch = Rachel (along with Sarah, Rebecca, Leah)

Patron saint of married women = Monica

Candle keeper = Chandler

These are five of the main characters in the NBC sitcom *Friends*. Joey is the missing character (a young kangaroo). And the coffee shop is Central Perk!

**27**   900 blue, 700 yellow, 850 red and 250 purple.

Gusharon sows 1,000 bulbs of each colour (4,000 in total).

Let's say the number of blue bulbs eaten by the worm is B. The number of yellow bulbs eaten is three times the blue ($3 \times B$). The number of red bulbs eaten is half the yellow ($1.5 \times B$). The number of purple bulbs eaten is five times the red ($7.5 \times B$).

The total number of bulbs eaten will be $B + 3B + 1.5B + 7.5B = 13 \times B$

If 2,700 bulbs will flower, that means 1,300 will be eaten ($4,000 - 2,700$), so $B = 1,300/13 = 100$. So, the bulbs eaten will be 100 blue, 300 yellow, 150 red and 750 purple.

**28**   Yes. $2018 = 503 + 504 + 505 + 506$.

To see where the answer comes from, let's first consider why at least four numbers are required. We can observe that the sum of two consecutive numbers is odd but 2018 is even, so at least three numbers are required. However, the sum of three consecutive numbers is a multiple of 3, and 2018 doesn't divide by 3. So at least four numbers are required. Their average should be $2018/4 = 504.5$, which leads us to find the stated numbers.

**29**  Only if it's February and not a leap year.

After the first day the population will fall to 10,000 × 99/100 = 9,900

After the second day the population will fall to 9,900 × 98/100 = 9,702

After 28 days the population falls to 10,000 × 99/100 × 98/100 × 97/100 × 96/100 × 95/100 × 94/100 × ... × 73/100 × 72/100 = 110

After 29 days it will fall to 110 × 71/100 = 78.

So, for months over 28 days there will be fewer than 100 spiders left and he won't get his funding.

**30**  Yes, it is possible. To do this, fold the ribbon in two at the midway point to get a doubled-up ribbon of length 72cm. Now double this again in the same way to get a folded ribbon of length 36cm. Repeat this process to obtain a folded ribbon of length 18cm, and then again to obtain a length of 9cm. Unfolding the ribbon will show 15 equally spaced creases dividing it into 16 pieces, each 9cm long. Cutting along the third crease from either end of the ribbon produces a piece of ribbon of length 27cm.

**31**   2 in 3 chance (67 per cent).

The chance of the first carpet being from Soaring Mat is one-third (10 out of 30). However, because we've been told that the carpet has failed, this gives us a little more information.

The inspector is expecting 20 landings from Flying Rug, with two in ten failures – i.e. four failures from Flying Rug. He is expecting ten landings from Soaring Mat, with eight in ten failures – i.e. eight failures from Soaring Mat. So, 12 failures are expected today, eight of which will be from Soaring Mat.

We know that this first landing has resulted in a failure, so the chance that it's a Soaring Mat carpet is 8 in 12, or 2 in 3.

**32**   Assuming that the Chancellor of the Exchequer knows how to add, they should find that the sum of the digits of the public debt is 1,000.

To see why, observe that we get the same total by adding all the digits of the one hundred numbers between 100 and 199.

Each number between 0 and 9 appears ten times as a third digit (following each of 10, 11, ... 19).
This contributes $10 \times (0 + 1 + 2 + ... + 9) = 10 \times 45 = 450$ to the total.

Each number between 0 and 9 also appears ten times as second digit (followed by 0, 1, ... 9), contributing another 450 to the total.

1 is the first digit 100 times, contributing 100 to the total.

So the grand total is $450 + 450 + 100 = 1,000$.

**33**   71.25 per cent (just over 7 out of 10).

We know that 10 per cent fail both at the first attempt, so we can ignore these students. 40 per cent will pass both and be admitted straight away. This leaves 50 per cent, split equally between students who need to re-sit statistics and those who need to re-sit finance (25 per cent each).

For those re-sitting statistics, three in four pass (75 per cent). From the original group it's 25 per cent × 75 per cent = 18.75 per cent.

For those resitting finance, one in two pass (50 per cent). From the original group it's 25 per cent × 50 per cent = 12.5 per cent.

Add these together: 40 per cent + 18.75 per cent + 12.50 per cent = 71.25 per cent.

**34**   Yes you can. Every number between 1 and 32 has a unique six-digit binary string that represents the number (000001, 000010, 000011 ... 011111, 100000). So, to find the number I'm thinking of, you can ask in turn whether the first/second/third/fourth/fifth binary digit (counted from the right) is zero.

**35**  45mph.

We can use the following equation:

distance travelled in miles = (average speed in miles per hour) × (time travelled in hours)

Letting $d$ be the distance between your home and work, and $t$ be the time spent going into work in the morning, we find that $d = 30 \times t$

The time taken to return home from work was ⅓ hours, because you travelled three times as fast. So, the total distance to and from work is $2d$, and the total time spent travelling to and from work is $t + ⅓ = {}^{4}t/_{3}$. Using the formula that relates distance, time and average speed, we find that:

$2d$ = (average speed of return journey) × $({}^{4}t/_{3})$.

However, we have already found that $d = 30t$. So the average speed of your return journey in mph =

$$\frac{2d}{\left(\dfrac{4t}{3}\right)} = \frac{2 \times 30t}{\dfrac{4t}{3}} = \frac{2 \times 30t \times 3}{4t} = 45.$$

**36**  Split the four coins into two separate piles of two coins, then choose one of the piles at random and turn both coins over to show the other side. One of three possibilities will have occurred:

- The two coins in the pile that you turned over were both heads-up, in which case, after the coins are flipped both piles now have no heads-up coins.

- One of the coins in the pile you turned over was heads-up, in which case, after the coins are flipped both piles now have one heads-up coin.

- Neither of the coins in the pile you turned over were heads-up, in which case, after the coins are flipped both piles now have two heads-up coins.

In all cases, the two piles you formed have the same number of heads-up coins.

**37**  Your friend's pension fund is now worth £50 because their cash sum of £1 is now worth 2 per cent of their pension fund.

**38** Anticlockwise. $8 \times 11 = 1 + (3 \times 29)$, so $16 \times 11 = 2 + (6 \times 29)$ is two more than a multiple of 29, which suggests taking the clockwise train and alighting the sixteenth time it stops. But if I then stayed on for another 13 stops, I would have gone $(16 + 13) \times 11 = 29 \times 11$ stations, and would be back at the start. So, I can get to where I want to be more efficiently by taking the anticlockwise train and getting off the thirteenth time it stops.

**39** Five days.

Each child can build a shrine in two years, or half a shrine in a year. Together, the 102 children would complete $102/2 = 51$ shrines in a year. You and your partner would each complete a shrine in a year, so working together could complete two shrines in a year. Likewise, your two parents could complete $2 \times 2$ shrines in a year, and your four grandparents $4 \times 4$ shrines in a year.

So, all working together you could build $51 + 2 + 4 + 16 = 73$ shrines in a year. There are 365 days in a non-leap year, and $365/73 = 5$.

**40** Yes, all the lemmings will eventually fall off the beam. To see why, consider the points on the beams occupied by the lemmings, rather than the lemmings themselves. The effect of two lemmings bumping into one another and turning around on the points occupied by the lemmings is the same as if the lemmings just walk through each other!

**41**   I am Sabine.

Sabine's journey is as follows:

210 miles takes three hours
45 minutes charging
Next 210 miles takes three hours
Total time = 6 hours and 45 minutes

Chris's journey is as follows:
60mph
420 miles
Total time = 7 hours

So Sabine arrives first even with a 45-minute break.

**42**   I in 27. For each mutation of a letter there are three possible alternatives and two letters that are mutated. In addition, there are three ways of pairing any two letters in a three-letter word. Therefore, the probability is given by $(1/3)^3 = 1/27$

An alternative way to tackle this problem is to list all the possible changes from ATG by changing any two of the letters. Start with ATG and change two of the letters:

AAA, AGA, ACA, AAT, AGT, ACT, AAC, AGC, ACC

TTA, TTT, TTC, GTA, GTT, GTC, CTA, CTT, CTC

TAG, TGG, TCG, GAG, GGG, GCG, CAG, CGG, CCG

There are 27 possibilities, one of which is TAG.

**43**   I have an identical twin who is the father of my nephew.

**44**   12 minutes.

The shearing time is related to the surface area of the sheep – the bigger the area to shear, the longer it takes. The surface area of a sphere (which we take to be the shape of a sheep) is proportional to the square of its radius.

And so with Dylan being twice as wide as Heather, his surface area is 4 times ($2^2$) the surface area of Heather. It thus takes 4 times as long to shear Dylan than it does Heather: 12 minutes. (This is highly idealised, especially as the real Heather only has three legs and hates the shearing process, and the real Dylan is so massive that shearing him is utterly exhausting. In reality I am pleased if I have sheared either of them within 20 minutes!).

**45**   The two large eggs.

One can find this by looking at all possible combinations of eating eggs within the six-minute window of opportunity:

six small eggs (6S) gives six units of chocolate
four small eggs and one medium egg (4S + 1M) give six units of chocolate
two small eggs and two medium eggs (2S + 2M) give six units of chocolate
three medium eggs (3M) give six units of chocolate
one large, 1 medium and 1 small egg (1L + 1M + 1S) give seven units of chocolate and two large eggs (2L) give 8 units of chocolate.

All times taken here are six minutes long.

**46**   3 in 5 (60 per cent). After picking the first glove, of the five gloves remaining, three would complete the pair (for instance, if the first glove I took was a left glove then among the five remaining there are still three right gloves). So there's a 3 in 5 chance I'll pick one to make up the pair.

**47**   7. In the first hour 8 eggs hatch and half of the ducklings (4) are eaten.

In the second hour 8 more ducklings hatch to join the remaining 4 ducklings, making 12 in total. But the fox eats half (6) of them.

In the third hour 8 more ducklings hatch, joining the remaining 6, making a total of 14.

But again the hungry fox gobbles up half of those, leaving only 7 left... Lucky old fox.

**48**   30%.

There are six ways in which eggs can be selected so that each of the three hens has contributed an egg to the omelette. Denoting the hens by T, O and G, the possible combinations for selecting the eggs are as follows:

TOG

TGO

OTG

OGT

GTO

GOT

Taking the first possibility (TOG), it can be calculated that there is a one in six chance of selecting Tilly's egg first, then a two in five chance of selecting one of Olivia's two eggs from the remaining five eggs, and then a three in four probability of selecting one of Gillian's three eggs from the remaining four eggs.

And so the probability of that combination is: $1/6 \times 2/5 \times 3/4 = 6/120 = 1/20 = 5\%$.

Fortunately calculating the probability of any one of these 6 events is the same, (e.g. GOT is $3/6 \times 2/5 \times 1/4 = 5\%$). And so the probability of selecting three eggs each laid by a different hen, is 6 times 5% = 30%.

**49** Horsham – Worthing – Brighton – Haywards Heath – Three Bridges – Redhill – Dorking – Horsham – Three Bridges.

The crew can't leave the tracks and they have to traverse all the lines, so when they're on a track that leads in to station A, for example, they have to take a track that exits from station A, unless A is the beginning or end of their trip. If a station appears an odd number of times in the full list, it has to be the beginning or ending station, otherwise they would enter a station but not be able to leave through a track they haven't used before.

Middle stations, such as Worthing in the route Brighton – Worthing – Horsham, count twice, as the route breaks down as Brighton – Worthing and Worthing – Horsham.

The only stations that appear an odd number of times are Horsham (three times) and Three Bridges (three times). So one of these stations must be the start and the other the end. From there you can work out the route.

If you look at the rail network map, you might be able to identify the solution simply by trying to drawing the route without lifting pencil from paper!

**50** The answers spell out the word DAHL:
Danny (the champion of the world)
Alfie (the tortoise in *Esio Trot*)
Miss Honey (the teacher from Matilda)
Lavender (Matilda's best school friend).

**51**     Eight times larger. The formula for the volume of a sphere is $4/3 \times \pi r^3$.
The key component is the $r$ cubed. This question is about scale factors.
We have a radius of 1, which is doubled to 2. The volume of the second
sphere is $2 \times 2 \times 2 = 8$.

**52**     6.28m. Counterintuitively, the answer would be the same for the Sun, the
Moon – any other planet or indeed a sphere of any size.

The maths requires the formula for circumference: $C = 2\pi \times$ radius.

The additional bit of rope ($h$) makes the new radius $R = r + h$, so: $C = 2\pi$
$\times (r + h) = 2\pi \times r + 2\pi \times h$.

The length of the rope at ground level is equal to Uranus's circumference:
$C = 2\pi \times r$.

The length of the rope raised above the ground by any height $h$:
$C = 2\pi (R(\text{original}) + h) = 2\pi \times R(\text{original}) + 2\pi \times h$

As the first part is the circumference of Uranus, the new part is $2\pi \times h$.

As $h = 1$m, the additional length required is $2\pi \times h = 2 \times 3.14 \times 1 = 6.28$.

**53**     21. The orchestra follows the Fibonacci sequence of 1, 1, 2, 3, 5, 8, 13...,
where a number is found by adding the two numbers before it. So the
next number in the sequence is $8 + 13 = 21$ violins.

**54**   Ten. To find the answer you could label her friends ABCDE and list all the different combinations. Alternatively, you can use a combination formula to work out the number of ways to select three friends out of five. Mathematically, the notation is $C(5,3) = 5!/(3!(5-3)!) = 10$ (Note: ! means factorial, so $3! = 3 \times 2 \times 1 = 6$).

**55**   1.381 per cent.

Let R = average growth rate.
The equation to set up is: 7.6 billion $\times R^{20} = 10$ billion.
We can use trial-and-error or logarithms. If we use logarithms, then the steps are:

**STEP 1:** $7.6 \times R^{20} = 10$
**STEP 2:** $R^{20} = 10/7.6$
**STEP 3:** Take the natural logarithm of both sides: $\log (R^{20}) = \log (10/7.6)$
**STEP 4:** $20 \log (\text{rate}) = \log (10/7.6)$
**STEP 5:** $\log (\text{rate}) = 1/20 \times \log (10/7.6)$
**STEP 6:** Take the exponential of both sides to get 1.013816419.

However, as an annual percentage rate, this is 1.381 per cent.

**56**   Ten hours. The circumference of the Earth is 40,000km, so the ten-hour flight is one quarter of the Earth's circumference. Singapore is approximately on the equator, as is Equatorial Guinea. Ten hours north from both places gets you to the North Pole.

**57** At the end of day eight. After eight days, sample A is $1 \times 1.2^8 = 4.30$g; sample B is $2 \times 1.1^8 = 4.29$g.

**58** 27,000km/h and 1.5 hours. The ratio of heights is 30 to 1, so the ratio of apparent speeds is the same. That means the speed of the ISS is about 27,000km/h. The circumference of Earth is about 40,000km, so the time to travel this distance is therefore about 1.5 hours.

**59** Ten hours. Blake spends 40 per cent of the day on poetry and 25 per cent on printmaking, which adds up to 65 per cent. So, the remaining 35 per cent = 3.5 hours, which makes the total working day ten hours long.

**60** English = 10,000 and French = 4,000.

You can solve this through trial and error or by setting up a simultaneous equation where E = English and F = French:

Equation 1: E + F = 14,000
Equation 2: E = 2.5F

Substitute E = 2.5F into the first equation:
2.5F + F = 14,000
3.5F = 14,000
F = 4,000
And so E = 10,000.

**61** 40mph.

The average speed is the total distance travelled divided by the total time.

The time for the 30mph segment is 10/30 hours = 20 minutes and for the 60mph segment it's 10/60 hours = 10 minutes. The total time is therefore half an hour.

The total distance is 20 miles, so the average speed is 20/0.5 = 40mph.

The knee-jerk answer is 45mph, which would be right if the 30mph and 60mph segments were driven for equal *times*, not *distances*.

**62**   10.2m.

Note that I live in Cambridge where the latitude is 52.2° and we know the Earth's tilt is 23.5°.

If the flagpole is height H then the length of the midwinter shadow is H × tan(52.2+23.5). We're told the shadow is 40m long so H = 10.2m.

Check the length of the midsummer shadow = 10.2 × tan(52.2-23.5) = 5.6m, as given.

So why give the midsummer length in the puzzle? Well, it is possible to answer this puzzle without the Cambridge clue and by using the two lengths provided. Give it a go – exercise your algebra! You will discover that the shadow lengths given in the puzzle give you a latitude of 52.1° (near enough) and a pole height of 10.27m.

**63**   The number 93 has four factors: 1, 3, 31 and 93. If you add these up you obtain 128. One interesting feature of 128 is that it can be written as $2^7$. However, it is also the largest number which cannot be expressed as the sum of distinct squares.

**64**   Archimedes' principle. A canal bridge carries its own weight and the weight of water that it contains. According to Archimedes' principle, when the floating barge is on the bridge, it displaces an amount of water equal to its own weight, so no matter how heavy it is, the barge makes no difference to the total loading of the bridge.

**65**   It's better to run on the bits in between the walkways.

Suppose I double my walking speed (*V*) when running (2*V*). By running on normal ground I halve the time taken for a given distance. If the moving walkway is also moving at my walking pace (*V*), for example, running on the walkway instead of walking would increase my speed from 2*V* to 3*V*, so that the time taken for a given distance is reduced to two-thirds of what it was. So by running for one minute on terra firma I'll get to the gate one minute quicker, while running for one minute on the walkway would only save me 30 seconds.

There's also the *reductio ad absurdum* argument. Suppose the walkways are super fast and you get to the end of each one in a very short time. Most of your journey is taken up by walking on ordinary ground, where running makes a real difference, but running on the walkways isn't going to have much effect because it's a small time anyway.

**66**   Yes. The wobblier track is the front wheel because that's the steering. The rear wheel follows on rather like a trailer on a car. I would be able to see that the rear wheel track goes over the front wheel track. Looking at the rear-wheel track, it can't know in advance what the front wheel will do. For example, if the bike does a right turn then the front wheel turns right and the rear wheel catches up. If I saw the rear wheel doing something before the front wheel, I'll know I've got the wrong direction.

**67**    30 per cent.

Draw a diagram of the three concentric orbits. Assume that Earth stays fixed at $\theta = 0$. With Mars at $\theta = 0$ then Venus is always further away. When Mars is at $\theta = 60°$ then Venus spends half its time nearer and half further away. You can check this with a bit of Pythagoras if you draw suitable 3:4:5 right-angled triangles. When Mars is at $\theta = 90°$ you'll find that Venus is always closer (more 3:4:5 Pythagoras). Put these together (sketch a graph) and it's clear that Mars is closer for at least 25 per cent of the time, so 30 per cent is a good guess.

**68**    £24. You can set up a simple simultaneous equation where A = adult and C = child:

$3A + 2C = 63$

$2A + 2C = 48$

One adult costs £15 (£63 − £48). So substituting £15 into the second equation gives 30 + 2C = 48. This means that two children cost £18, so one child costs £9. £15 + £9 = £24.

**69**  38 per cent and I per cent. There are eight outcomes. 0 is OK and f is fail:

000   $0.8 \times 0.8 \times 0.8 = 0.512$
00f   $0.8 \times 0.8 \times 0.2 = 0.128$
0f0   $0.8 \times 0.2 \times 0.8 = 0.128$
0ff   $0.8 \times 0.2 \times 0.2 = 0.032$
f00   $0.2 \times 0.8 \times 0.8 = 0.128$
f0f   $0.2 \times 0.8 \times 0.2 = 0.032$
ff0   $0.2 \times 0.2 \times 0.8 = 0.032$
fff   $0.2 \times 0.2 \times 0.2 = 0.008$

So by adding up:
No engines failing = 51 per cent
One engine failing = 38 per cent
Two engines failing. = 10 per cent
Three engines failing = 1 per cent.

**70**  MY = Malaysia.

Valletta is the capital of Malta. The actor who starred as Willy Wonka is Gene Wilder. If you cross out the letters from the words Malta and Wilder from Walter Mildmay, you have M and Y remaining. This forms the two-letter ISO code for Malaysia.

**71**  Nine classes with 23 students in each. 207 can be written as I × 207, 3 × 69 or 9 × 23. The last is the only reasonable answer for classes in a school.

**72**   16. You can use trial and error or algebra to set up an equation to work this out.

B picked up $x$ bricks. A picked up $2x$ bricks. C picked up $2x - 4$ bricks.

$x + 2x + (2x - 4) = 36$

$5x - 4 = 36$

$5x = 40$

$x = 8$

Knowing that Robot B picked up eight bricks, you can work out Robot A's bricks by doubling that.

**73**   The greater volume can be achieved by curving the paper along the long side.

A4 measurements are 210mm × 297mm. The volume of a cylinder is $\pi$ × radius × radius × height, where the radius = circumference/($2\pi$).

Volume folded along the short side (circumference = 210mm; height = 297mm):
Volume = $\pi$ × (210/$2\pi$) × (210/$2\pi$) × 297
= (210 × 210 × 297)/(2 × $2\pi$)
= 3,274,425/$\pi$

Volume folded along the long side (circumference = 297mm; height = 210mm):
Volume = $\pi$ × (297/$2\pi$) × (297/$2\pi$) × 210
= (297 × 297 × 210)/(2 × $2\pi$)
= 4,360,972.5/$\pi$

**74**   5. A = 1, B = 2, C = 3 and so on. 7 – 3 – 19 can be interpreted as G – C – S. The code word is GCSE, hence the missing letter is E, represented by the number 5.

**75**   Three. Between 1820 and 1821, between 8201 and 8202, and 2018 itself.

**76**   3,456. There are 6 ways to choose the seats occupied by the Indigos, 24 ways to arrange the Indigos, and 24 ways to arrange the Violets. 6 × 24 × 24 = 3,456.

**77**   18. She made a 6 × 3 rectangle.

Call the length x and width y, with $x > y$. For the area and perimeter to be equal, then $xy = 2x + 2y$, so $(x - 2)(y - 2) = 4$. The only whole number solution is $x = 6$, $y = 3$. Hence 18 tiles were used.

**78**   Dustin, Angelina and Charlize were telling the truth.

**79**   -12.

Let n be the original number displayed. Suppose that after X and Y are pressed once each, the number displayed is equal to n. Then after ten presses each, the number displayed will again be n.

To find this number, we can solve $n/4 - 9 = n$ to obtain $n = -12$.

To see why no other number works after ten presses each, notice that n must satisfy a (complicated) linear equation, which can only have one solution. Since we know that $n = -12$ works, this is the only solution.

**80**   9, 10 and 11.

**81**   56p and 28p. Many people will try and guess the answer, but some will realize that the boy has two-thirds of 84p and his friend has one-third.

**82**   Two minutes. Many will say five minutes but each child eats an ice cream in two minutes.

**83**  Six and eleven years old. Some people will try random guesses, which will modify if the total is incorrect.

One method is to subtract 5 from the total sum, and then halve it to find the brother's age.

Another method is to halve the total sum, add 2.5 to find the girl's age and subtract 2.5 to get the brother's age.

**84**  Fill the 3-litre jug and pour all the contents into the 5-litre jug. Fill the 3-litre jug again and, from it, fill up the 5 litre jug. One litre remains in the 3-litre jug.

**85**  No direction – it's an electric train.

**86**  175 and 143. Take 32 from the total of 318 and divide by two to get the lower number of votes (143). Then add 32 back to that to get 175.

**87**   24 is the smallest number of tiles required to make four different rectangles. This could take a long time unless you examine numbers quickly, listing possible factors. Prime numbers should be quickly dismissed and numbers with many factors recognized and examined more closely.

36 is the smallest number of tiles required to make five different rectangles. Remember that squares are particular cases of rectangles.

**88**   1p and 23p. At first glance this appears impossible, but further thought leads you to deduce that the child with less money must have 1p and the packet of sweets must cost 25p.

**89**   They are the same distance from London when they cross! The speeds, times and distances from London are not needed to find this answer. Instead, you can draw a distance–time graph, and the intersection will tell you the approximate time the trains crossed, as well as the approximate distance from London. That way you can avoid tedious algebra, which would give a time of 2 hours and 56 minutes and a distance of 205.3 miles from London for both trains.

**90**   There were nine runners and I finished fourth. You can deduce that the number of runners must be odd, because in the first situation there are equal numbers of runners in front and behind. Examining all odd numbers starting at 3 will give the answer.

**91**  Mother = £13.50. Son = £8.50. Daughter = £6.50.

Looking at the first two statements, you can deduce that the son has £2 more than the daughter, which means, looking at the final statement, that you need to split £15 into two parts so that one part is £2 more than the other. The parts cannot be whole numbers – they have to be £8.50 and £6.50.

**92**  Nine days. If it doubles its size every day and fills the box at ten days, then at nine days it will be half the size it is at ten days, thus filling half the box.

**93**  1,050. The calculation is: 5 + (5 × 11) + (5 × 11 × 18) = 1,050.

**94**  165°. The angle between each full number on a clock face is 30°, so between the 6 and the 11 is 150°. Then add 15° because the little hand is halfway between the 11 and 12.

**95**  It is a prime number (173). Adding up the numbers in National Puzzle Day gives 222. Adding up the numbers in 29/01/19 gives 49. The answer is therefore 222 − 49 = 173.

**96**   31 per cent. The easiest way to solve this is to first determine the probability that *none* of the replacements would fail in this time. This is given by 89 per cent × 89 per cent × 93 per cent × 93 per cent = 0.89 × 0.89 × 0.93 × 0.93 = 0.69, or 69 per cent.

So, the probability that anything else happens is 100 per cent − 69 per cent = 31 per cent. Given the scale of the procedure you've had, that seems pretty good!

**97**   The octahedron.

If there are any vertices with three or five edges that meet, then that vertex must be the start or the finish of your finger's journey, because you need an even number at a junction to give you an entrance and an exit.

If there are more than two 'odd' vertices on the object then the lift-free journey is impossible. The tetrahedron, cube, dodecahedron and icosahedron are made up of triangles, squares or pentagons, and all the vertices are odd meetings of edges. But all six vertices of an octahedron are meetings of four edges. This makes it possible to trace out a path in many different ways. It is one of the only 3D solids that can have its edges traced like this. Can you think of any others? I can only think of other base-to-base pyramids, which is a bit boring!

**98**   The oldest pirate should propose a 98 : 0 : 1 : 0 : 1 split. That is, he (the oldest pirate) would get 98 coins, the middle pirate gets 1 coin and the youngest gets 1 coin. To see how it works, consider the pirates A, B, C, D and E, from oldest to youngest. Working backwards:

If there were only two pirates: D splits the coins D = 100 : E = 0 (giving himself all the gold). His vote (50 per cent) is enough to ensure the deal.

If there were only three pirates: C splits the coins C = 99 : D = 0 : E = 1. E will accept this deal (getting just 1 coin), because he knows that if he rejects it there will be only two pirates left, and he gets nothing.

If there were only four pirates: B splits the coins B = 99 : C = 0 : D = 1 : E = 0. By the same reasoning as before, D will accept this deal.

With five pirates: A splits the coins A = 98 : B = 0 : C = 1 : D = 0 : E = 1. By offering a gold coin to C and a gold coin to E (who would otherwise get nothing) he is assured of a deal.

**99**   120° or 80°. The angles are A, A and B.

If B is the largest then B = 4 × A and A + A + B = 180°
So 6 × A = 180°
A = 30° and B = 120°.

If A is the largest then A = 4 × B and A + A + B = 180°
So 9 × B = 180°
B = 20° and A = 80°.

**100** About £425,000.

Susan's salary is £50,000, which will grow each year by 3 per cent. So next year her salary will be 50,000 × 1.03 (£51,500) and the following year 51,500 × 1.03 (£53,045). By the time she reaches 65 this will have grown 20 times (50,000 × $1.03^{20}$ = 90,306), so her target pension is half that: £45,153. So, the fund she'd need at age 65 is 25 × 45,153 = 1,128,825.

However, as she's investing the money now – 20 years before the event – in a fund that is expected to grow by 5 per cent each year, she can hold less than this.

If she invested the money one year before retirement, she would need 1,128,825/1.05 = 1,075,071. If she was investing it two years before retirement, she'd need 1,075,071/1.05 = 1,023,878. But here she's investing it 20 years before retirement so she needs to set aside 1,128,825 divided by 1.05 20 times = 425,442, which rounds to 425,000.

**101** As this is a book, the two leaves will have four separate and consecutive page numbers. Let's call x the first missing page. Then the next three are x + 1, x + 2 and x + 3.

x + (x + 1) + (x + 2) + (x + 3) = 82
4x + 6 = 82
4x = 76
x = 19

So the page numbers are 19, 20, 21 and 22.

**102** 1.8 per cent (less than 1 in 50 chance).

If we look at the combinations, we can see that in order to reach £20,000, Sid needs his fund to grow by 7 per cent in at least five of the six years:

$14,000 \times 1.07 \times 1.07 \times 1.07 \times 1.07 \times 1.07 \times 1.03 = 20,225$.

Anything less than that won't return enough:

$14,000 \times 1.07 \times 1.07 \times 1.07 \times 1.07 \times 1.03 \times 1.03 = 19,469$.

So, we need to look at the probabilities of having 7 per cent growth in all six years and also in five out of six years.

In any one year, the probability of getting 7 per cent is 1/3 and of getting 3 per cent is 2/3 (we know this because the probability of 3 per cent is twice that of 7 per cent).

The probability of getting 7 per cent in all six years is $1/3 \times 1/3 \times 1/3 \times 1/3 \times 1/3 \times 1/3 = 0.001372$.

The probability of getting 7 per cent in five years and 3 per cent in one is $1/3 \times 1/3 \times 1/3 \times 1/3 \times 1/3$ (five years of getting 7 per cent) $\times 2/3$ (one year of getting 3 per cent). However, we also need to multiply this by the number of possible combinations, which is six (the year of 3 per cent can be the first, second, third, fourth, fifth or sixth year), which gives us $1/3 \times 1/3 \times 1/3 \times 1/3 \times 1/3 \times 2/3 \times 6 = 0.016461$.

Add these two together and we get 0.017833 – i.e. about 0.018 which is 1.8 per cent (which is less than 1 in 50 chance).

**103**  353cm$^2$ rounded answer (your answer may vary slightly depending on what value of π you use).

The can has two circles, each with an area of π x radius x radius = 2 x (3.14 x 3.8 x 3.8) = 90.68cm$^2$

The curved surface area is π x diameter x height = 3.14 x 7.6 x 11 = 262.50cm$^2$

Total area = 45.34 + 262.50 = 353.18cm$^2$

**104**  Teachers = 5
Parents = 10
Children = 20.

You can set up a simple ratios question. Call teachers T. Then parents are 2T and children are 4T.

T + 2T + 4T = 7T = 35. Then T = 5.

**105** For the shopping list, Bobby and Rachel need four bottles of wine and five pizzas.

Which deal is better? Rachel's is equivalent to 1/3 off, while Bobby's is only equivalent to 3/10 off. So Rachel should buy as much as possible:

Wine Wine (free Wine) Pizza Pizza (free Pizza)
WWw PPp
Cost = 15 + 15 + 0 + 8 + 8 + 0 = £46.

Bobby and Rachel still need one bottle of wine and two pizzas. For this, it is better to use Bobby's 30% off:

Cost of Wine Pizza Pizza = 15 + 8 + 8 = £31
30% reduction from £31 gives Bobby £21.70 cost

So the cheapest is for Rachel to buy 3 bottles of wine and 3 pizzas (paying for just 2 and 2) at £46. Then Bobby buys 1 bottle of wine and 2 pizzas at £21.70. So £67.70 in total.

**106** 14 days.

279 episodes x 20 minutes = 5580 minutes in total

5580 minutes / 60 = 93 hours total to watch

For a 9am–5pm slot, there are 7 working hours.

With 7 hours per day, 93 hours / 7 hours = 13.29 days.

So they will need 14 days to complete the series.

**107** Five. This is a version of a classic SAT multiple-choice question where the examiners didn't actually include the correct answer!

Most people will instinctively say four. To work out where that extra revolution fits in, imagine there are two circles of the same radius, for example two 10p coins. If we use the same gut instinct, we would say that coin A should only revolve once as it rolls around coin B, but let's see…

If we position them so that the Queen's head is upright on both and start to roll coin A around coin B, by the time coin A has rolled half way around coin B the Queen's head will be upright to the viewer. (If you don't believe me, try it!) Once it reaches its starting point again, it will have completed another full revolution, so the answer for circles of the same radius is two.

Back to our problem. Although the circumference of circle A is a quarter of circle B, the fact that A's journey is itself a circle rather than a straight line means that to the viewer there will always be one more revolution than instinct might initially suggest.

**108** 1 cm. The amount used halfway through is proportional to the loss of cross-sectional area, which is $\pi (7^2 - 5^2) = \pi (49 - 25) = 24\pi$ (in cm$^2$). In using it up, I must lose another $24\pi$ cm$^2$, getting from $25\pi$ cm$^2$ down to $1\pi$ cm$^2$, so the radius of the tube is 1 cm.

**109** Five in seven. This is really a question about the equilibrium distribution of a Markov chain.

Think of a particular new member of the Magenta party, such as the first one after 1 March. Let $b$ be the probability that they are an ex-Blue and $r$ for a former Red.

The probability that the second new member after 1 March comes from the Blue party is $b \times 9/10 + r \times 1/4$. However, this must also be equal to $b$. Therefore $r = 0.4 b$. Since they sum to 1, we must have $b = 5/7$, $r = 2/7$. So, in the long run, five in seven Magenta party members used to be Blues.

**110** Six. It is easier to get to two than one as there are two routes: two direct (1 in 6 chance) and one then one (1 in 36 chance). By extension, it is easier to get to three than two, four than three, five than four and six than five.

There is no direct route to numbers seven and greater, but it is certain that there will be a first time you are within six of any such larger number, so the chance of hitting a number greater than six is a weighted average of the chances of hitting each of the numbers one to six. Therefore it cannot be more likely than the most likely of the numbers one to six. So the best number to pick is six.

**111**   Nine, two and two.

To begin with, break down all the possible combinations:

36, 1, 1 (improbable!)

18, 2, 1 (at best unlikely)

12, 3, 1

9, 2, 2

6, 6, 1

6, 3, 2

9, 4, 1

Two sets (9, 2, 2 and 6, 6, 1) have identical sums, which is why the colleague could not deduce their ages from the passing house until he learned that the *eldest* was taking piano lessons. 6, 6, 1 does not have an eldest, so the answer must be 9, 2, 2.

**112**   2.56 per cent. Solve $(1 + i)^{365} = 1,000,000/100$.

**113** D: More than 4 per cent (about 4.7 per cent in this case, both brothers repay their loan in year 30).

You need a spreadsheet to get the exact number, but the logic here is that the first brother is getting extra value by paying down the outstanding loan because not only is he unwinding a debt at 4 per cent, but he's bringing forward the point where he only pays 2 per cent. You can improve on this further by paying down the loan until you reach the lower rate of interest and then using the savings account if the net rate of interest is greater than the lower rate of the interest on the mortgage.

**114** 216 years. The moons are at distances 1, 4 and 9 from the planet. According to Kepler's law, the duration of orbit is therefore in a ratio of 1:8:27. The lowest common multiple of 1, 8 and 27 is 216.

**115** 16. Divide the grid into blocks of three by two. The line goes through four of these blocks and crosses four squares in each.

**116**  The fund manager.

At 0 per cent interest: £10,896 v. £7,900.

At 5 per cent interest: £36,314 v. £17,321 (assumes the fund manager's fees are then invested at same rate of interest).

The fund manager takes 1 per cent of the £1,000 in the first year. In the second year he takes 1 per cent of £1,000 *plus* 1 per cent of the first year's £1,000. After 50 years, he has taken 1 per cent of the first contribution 50 times.

**117**  50 per cent. Four mistakes has a chance of 5/32. No mistakes has a chance of 1/32 and two mistakes has a chance of 10/32.

**118**  Player B is favourite to win, by approximately 3 to 1.

Player A has a roughly 50:50 chance of hitting 99 or 100, but if he hits 99 then he is stuck because he can never roll a 1.

It is possible to rearrange the snakes and ladders so that the converse result applies, but this would require something like putting six snakes in a row so that player B could never pass them.

You really need to use a computer and simulate thousands of games to work this out. In theory, you could work out a closed form solution but it would be extremely complicated. In practice the arrangement of snakes and ladders makes very little difference. This answer was worked out for a standard board using a Monte Carlo calculation in which the game was simulated thousands of times to see who actually won.

**119**  Yes, it is possible. Imagine four copies of the given sheet, each with 100 coins placed to form a rectangle whose sides are double those of the original sheet. This new rectangle has 400 coins of 2cm diameter on it. Now shrink this large sheet (with the coins) by a factor of two to the size of the original rectangle. The 400 coins now have a diameter of 1cm as required, with no overlapping.

**120** Start with the goblin furthest from its nearest neighbour, say goblin B. If B's nearest goblin is A, then they form a pair that can be eliminated, reducing the problem to nine goblins. Proceed by recursion. For odd numbers of goblins such as 11, the recursion stops before or at three. In the latter case, without loss of generality, the distance ranking is AB < AC < BC, and C remains dry. If B's nearest goblin is not A, then B is nearer to other goblins and A will be remain dry.

**121** Yes. There are seven possible rotations of the table including the initial one in which no one has their own dish. By rotating the table, each of the seven diners has their own dish in at least one of the other six rotations. Since seven is greater than six, there is at least one rotation in which two (or more) diners will get their own dish.

**122** Instead of thinking of the 18 bottles, think of the 6 holes left without a bottle – the final answer will be the same.

As the question states, there needs to be an even number of holes in each row and column, i.e. 0, 2, 4 or 6. You will soon realise that you need zero or two holes in each row and each column, as having four or six holes does not work. The only way to have six holes in the crate with two holes in each row and column is to have a 3x3 arrangement, of the following form (or some arrangement of it), somewhere in the crate. Here, H represents one of the six holes, and a dash represents a bottle.

HH-
H-H
-HH

Note that the rows or columns do not need to be adjacent. If you try to arrange the six holes with two (or zero) in each row and column you always end up with an arrangement like this. We now just need to count the number of times these arrangements can occur.

For any particular choice of three rows and three columns there are six ways of allocating the six holes, with two holes in each row and each column, to six of the nine cavities. To see this, note that there are three ways of allocating the bottle in the top row, then two ways of allocating the bottle in the middle row and just one way of allocating the bottle in the bottom row.

There are four ways of choosing the three rows out of four, and twenty ways of selecting the three columns out of six. In total, we have:
$6 \times 4 \times 20 = 480$ ways of allocating the holes (and the same number of ways of allocating the 18 bottles).

**123** 6210001000. Notice that the sum of the digits of $N$ is ten – this limits some lines of enquiry.

First, try to find the number of 0s in $N$. It should become clear that seven, eight and nine don't work. Try six. If there are six 0s then there must be exactly one 6 in $N$ – there can't be more. In other words, the seventh digit of $N$ is a 1.

How many 1s are there in $N$? There can't be just one 1, otherwise the second digit would be a 1 and we would have at least two 1s, leading to a contradiction. So, suppose there are two 1s, making the second digit of $N$ a 2. The third digit of $N$ is then at least 1, but making it more than 1 doesn't work. Setting the third digit equal to 1 reveals the answer.

**124** As the first train leaves, Mo is left standing on the platform next to the rear of it. He runs down the platform and is in time to board the second train at the front. When he gets to his destination he is next to the exit, while some passengers from the first train are still walking the length of the platform to reach it.

**125** To show that this will always happen, start by choosing any one of the six points. The six lines you draw from this point will have at least three lines of the same colour. Look at the red lines and the points that connect them. If any two of these points are connected by a red line, then this would complete a red triangle. If this were not the case then a blue triangle would be created.

**126** 28 years. As there are four years between leap years and seven days in the week, the calendar is the same after 4 × 7 = 28 years.

Note: If the calendar was for a century year such as 2000, this would spoil the pattern, and would only repeat every 400 years!

**127** Ten.

Two ways: one face one colour + other five faces other colour
Four ways: two faces one colour + other four faces other colour
Four ways: three faces one colour + other three faces other colour

**128** Possible ways of making the integers:

$1 = (4 \div 4) + 4 - 4$

$2 = (4 \div 4) + (4 \div 4)$

$3 = (4 + 4 + 4) \div 4$

$4 = 4 + (4 - 4) \times 4$

$5 = (4 \times 4 + 4) \div 4$

$6 = 4 + (4 + 4) \div 4$

$7 = 4 + 4 - (4 \div 4)$

$8 = 4 + 4 + 4 - 4$

$9 = 4 + 4 + (4 \div 4)$

$10 = (44 - 4) \div 4$

$11 = (4 \div 0.4) + (4 \div 4)$

$12 = (4 - (4 \div 4)) \times 4$

$13 = (4! \times \sqrt{4} + 4) \div 4$

$14 = (4! \div 4) + 4 + 4$

$15 = 4 \times 4 - (4 \div 4)$

$16 = 4 \times 4 + (4 - 4)$

$17 = 4 \times 4 + (4 \div 4)$

$18 = 4 \times 4 + (4 \div \sqrt{4})$

$19 = 4! - 4 - (4 \div 4)$

$20 = ((4 \div 4) + 4) \times 4$

I'm sure you can think of different ways. If you like this puzzle, try making all the integers to 100 using four 4s!

**129** Yes. Pick up the second glass from the left and pour its contents into the fifth glass in the row. Then replace this glass in its original position.

**130** The husband is 44 years old and the wife 33 years old.

Possible solution:

Using the following letters, husband (H) and wife (W), you can write H + W = 77. For the younger ages, use husband (M) and for his wife (F). This results in:

H − W = M − F
H = 2F
M = W

Substituting for H = 2F and M = W in H − W = M − F gives 2F − W = W − F.

Therefore, we obtain this relationship between F and W:
3F = 2W.

Using this relationship with H = 2F and H + W = 77 gives an equation in terms of F:
2F + (3/2)F = 77

Solving this for F, obtain the equation 7F = 154 and so F = 22.

If F = 22, then H = 2 × 22 = 44 and W = 77 − 44 = 33.

**131**  Baby boy is 4kg and baby girl is 3kg. Using the following letters, baby boy (B) and baby girl (G), gives:

4G = 3B

G + B = 7

Using 4G = 3B we can write G = (3/4)B. Substituting this into G + B = 7 we obtain (3/4)B + B = 7.

Solving this equation gives 4B = 28, therefore B = 4. If B = 4, then G + 4 = 7, so G = 3.

**132**  Using a short straw (7–12cm), blow strongly across the top of coin. You will need to blow nearly horizontally across the top of the coin.

The coin will vibrate, jump and spin due to the pressure difference caused by moving air over its surface.

**133** 24, 18 and 12. Using the following letters, Eldest son (E), second son (S) and youngest son (Y), gives:

$E = S + 6$

$S = Y + 6$

$E = 2Y$

Substituting $E = 2Y$ and $S = Y + 6$ into $E = S + 6$ gives $2Y = (Y + 6) + 6$. Hence $Y = 12$.

We can then use this value of Y to find the other two ages.

$E = 2 \times 12 = 24$

$S = 12 + 6 = 18$

**134** Slowly and carefully slide the glass to the edge of the table. Allow the water to drain into another glass.

**135** £135.

Possible solution:

With money in your wallet (M), we can write $(1/3)M + (1/3)(2M/3) = 75$

Adding gives $(5/9)M = 75$ and $M = 135$.

Hence you would originally have £135 in your wallet.

**136** Seven. One way of working this out is: $7x + 13y = 1,000$. Rewrite this equation as: $x = (1,000 - 13y)/7 = 142 - y + (6 - 6y)/7$.

Let $P = (6 - 6y)/7$ and $y = 1 - P - P/6$. If we let $Q = P/6$ this gives $x = 141 + 13Q$ and $y = 1 - 7Q$.

| Q | y notebooks | x pens |
|---|---|---|
| 0 | 1 | 141 |
| -1 | 8 | 128 |
| -2 | 15 | 115 |
| -3 | 22 | 102 |
| -4 | 29 | 89 |
| -5 | 36 | 76 |
| -6 | 43 | 63 |
| -7 | 50 | 50 |

**137** Most people will write 'blue', 'triangle' and '37'.

There is a high likelihood that most people will choose the first two of these answers because of popular associations we have with sets of colours and shapes, with red and blue being the most popular primary colours.

When thinking about types of shapes, the first that come to mind are circle, square and triangle. As the question has suggested two of these answers already, people will select a different option.

Finally, for both digits to be odd, the choices are 13, 15, 17, 19, 31, 35 and 37. The wording of the question suggests that we should not select 15 or anything with a 1 and so we are left with 35 and 37. The digit 5 is already mentioned in the question, and generally, 7 is thought to be lucky, making 37 the most frequently selected number.

**138** 3/10 orange and 7/10 water.

The proportion of glasses with orange juice to the total mixture in the two glasses can be written as: (1/2) + (1/5)2 : 1 + 2., which simplifies to (1/6) + (2/15) : 1.

So, 1/6 of the small glass and 2/15 of the large glass are filled with orange juice. Simplifying this gives 9/30 (or 3/10) of the mixture as orange, leaving 21/30 (or 7/10) as water.

**139** Harry £150, Dick £170 and Tom £180. Using the following letters, with Tom (T), Dick (D) and Harry (H), gives:

T + D + H = 500
T = 10 + D
D = 20 + H

Substituting for D to give T = 10 + (20 + H) = 30 + H

We now have two equations in H and can use these together with T + D + H = 500 to obtain a value for H:

(30 + H) + (20 + H ) + H = 500, and so 3H = 450.

As H = 150, D = 20 + 150 = 170. Therefore T = 10 + 170 = 180.

This gives Harry £150, Dick £170 and Tom £180.

**140** Grumpy has 28 spots, Sneezy 14 spots and Happy 56 spots. One way of working this out is:

$G + S + H = 98$

$G = 2S$

$H = 2G$

$2S + S + 4S = 98$

So, $S = 14$ and $G = 2 \times 14 = 28$ and $H = 2 \times 28 = 56$.

**141** Peter is 20 and Tim is 10. One way of working this out is:

$P > T$

$P + T = 3(P - T)$ and so $2T = P$

$P = T + 10$, so $T = 10$

**142** Six different possible groups. One way of working this out is:

$6x + 5y = 171$

Rewrite this equation as:

$x = (171 - 5y)/6 = 28 + (3 - 5y)/6$

Let $P = (3 - 5y)/6$ and $y = -P + (3 - P)/5$

If we let $Q = (3 - P)/5$ this gives $x = 31 - 5Q$ and $y = 6Q - 3$.

| Q | y men | x women |
|---|-------|---------|
| 1 | 3     | 26      |
| 2 | 9     | 21      |
| 3 | 15    | 16      |
| 4 | 21    | 11      |
| 5 | 27    | 6       |
| 6 | 33    | 1       |

## **143** 3 in 7.

A good way to start on problems like these is to decide an efficient way of counting up the (equally likely) possibilities. Label the positions around the table from 1 to 8, with positions 1 and 8 adjacent (as it's a round table). We can also, for instance, assume, without losing generality, that a Remainer sits in position 1, and we can write this configuration as R _ _ _ _ _ _ _.

If deciding by lot, there are $(7 \times 6 \times 5)/(3 \times 2 \times 1) = 35$ equally likely possible combinations of seats that the rest of the Remainers can occupy.

They can all sit separately (RLRLRLRL), which can only happen one way, or all Remainers and Leavers can sit in pairs, which can happen in two ways (RRLLRRLL or RLLRRLLR).

However, it is also possible for the Remainers to sit as a pair and two singles (forcing the Leavers to do the same), and here there are a few more.

If the R in position 1 is part of the pair, then we have either RRL _ _ _ _ L or RL _ _ _ _ LR, and in each case there are three ways for the remaining Rs to sit as singles. Or the R in position 1 is a single, giving RL _ _ _ _ _ L, with the remaining Rs to be placed as a pair and a single. This can happen as RRLRL, RRLLR or LRRLR, or the same three combinations with the RR and R swapped. In total this gives 12 ways.

So altogether there are $1 + 2 + 12 = 15$ ways out of the 35, giving a probability of 3 in 7.

Which seems to suggest, in life, that echo chambers are more likely to form than not. Oh well.

**144** Proms 1 and 73.

I will certainly attend the First Night of the Proms, since 75 is divisible by 1. However, 75 is not divisible by 2, and having torn that card in half, there are now 76 pieces of card on the table. 76 is not divisible by 3, so that card is torn in half too, and so on.

We could continue checking by brute force, but at this stage you wonder just which is the first card to stay intact after card number 1; in other words, what is the least positive integer k, such that $75 + k - 1$ is divisible by $1 + k$?

This requires finding the positive integer solutions of $n(1 + k) = 74 + k$, which rearranges to $(n - 1)(k + 1) = 73$. Rather handily, 73 is a prime number, whose only factors are 1 and 73, so either $k = 0$ (the trivial solution) or $k = 72$, meaning that card number 73 is the next to survive. After that it is easy to check that cards 74 and 75 both get torn up. So I am going to Proms 1 and 73.

**145** The cucumber.

The dry mass of the cucumber (which doesn't evaporate) accounts for 5 per cent of the overall mass before and 8 per cent after. So, after sitting in the sun the cucumber has 5/8 of the mass it had originally. This is a loss of 37.5 per cent.

Similarly, the melon's dry mass accounts for 10 per cent of the overall mass before and 15 per cent after, so the melon has 2/3 of the mass it had originally, a loss of 33.3 per cent.

**146** $2.7 \times 10^{22} \times 10^{-3})/(2.6 \times 10^{19})$, which is about 1.

We first need to estimate the volume of the atmosphere. Assuming a height of 50km and taking the radius of Earth to be 6,400km, the volume is approximately $(50,000) \times 4 \times 3.14 \times (6,400,000)^2 = 2.6 \times 10^{19}m^3$.

The volume of air in a breath is approximately 1 litre ($10^{-3}m^3$). The volume of 1 mole of gas at atmosphere pressure and temperature is 22.4 litres. The number of molecules in one breath is $6 \times 10^{23} \times (1/22.4) = 2.7 \times 10^{22}$, where $6 \times 10^{23}$ is Avogadro's constant.

The number of molecules from Julius Caesar's last breath in $10^{-3}m^3$ of well-mixed air is just the number of molecules multiplied by the dilution ratio of $10^{-3}$/volume of the atmosphere, i.e. $2.7 \times 10^{22} \times 10^{-3})/(2.6 \times 10^{19})$, which is about 1.

**147** $7.5m^{-1}$ if you cut the ball up into segments like cheeses with three flat sides, with each cut perpendicular to each other.

Another way of cutting the ball into eight pieces yields $9m^{-1}$ – if you cut the ball into segments like an orange.

**148**   95 for men and 100 for women.

Well, if you are a male and are 79 today then your life expectancy is ... 79. Watch out! We know the life expectancy of someone born today can't be 79 + (79 × 2/12) = 92.17 years because at that age, your life expectancy will have increased to 79 + (92.17 × 2/12) = 94.36, and so on.

The best way to solve this is by saying life expectancy is $y$, so that $y = 79 + (y × 2/12)$ for men. We get $y = 94.8$ (i.e. about 95) years for men.

Using the same approach, we find that the life expectancy of a girl born today would be 99.6, i.e. about 100 years. Lots of letters from the monarch being written!

**149**   270m. The oceans cover approximately 70 per cent of Earth. The radius of Earth is 6,371km.

The area of the oceans is 70 per cent × 4 × P × 6,371km × 6,371km, which is approximately 357,000,000km². The volume of water we are dealing with is therefore (0.1/1000)km × 357,000,000km² = 35700km³.

The area of England is 130,279km². The height of water if spread just over England would therefore be 35,700/130,279 = 0.27km, or 270m.

**150** 16 years.

Let current population $= Y$.

Number of females $= Y/2$

The average number of births per year $= (Y/2) \times (1/80)$ (you can imagine that all women have their child at a given age to help arrive at this assumption)

Number of deaths per year $= Y/80$

Net change per year $= Y/160 - Y/80$, i.e. $-Y/160$

$-10 \times Y = -Yn/160$ (where $n$ is the number of years), so $n = 16$ years.

It is also possible to jump straight to the equation $10 = n/(2Q)$, where $Q$ is the life expectancy.

**151** $6,667. Half the time you buy one bitcoin at $10,000 each, and the other half of the time you buy two bitcoins at $5,000 each. So, after two months you have spent $20,000 and purchased three bitcoins. The average price of your purchase is therefore $20,000/3 = $6,667, which is less than half of the difference between $10,000 and $5,000 (i.e. $7,500). You buy at less than the average price.

**152** 13 per cent reduction. Assuming a domestic mouse is about 40g and is made basically from water (density 1000kg/m³), then the volume of the domestic mouse is 40/1,000,000m³ = 4 × 10⁻⁵m³.

The radius of the domestic mouse sphere is $\sqrt[3]{\dfrac{4\times10^{-5}}{4\pi/_3}}$ = 0.021m.

The radius of a super-sized mouse is $\sqrt[3]{\dfrac{1.5\times4\times10^{-5}}{4\pi/_3}}$ = 0.024m.

The ratio of surface area to volume of a sphere = 3/r. Therefore, the ratio of surface area to volume changes from 141m⁻¹ for the domestic mouse to 124m⁻¹ for the super-sized one, a reduction of 13 per cent.

**153**  About 2.24m.

If the ant is travelling along the path of shortest distance, then it will pass directly from a face connected to the corner it was standing at on to a face which is connected to their destination. The box can be cut and opened to form the cross shown below:

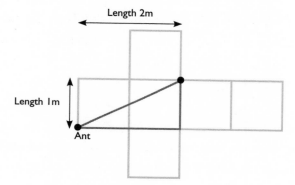

The distance of a path between two points on the box does not change when the sides are flattened out. So the minimum distance between two points on the flat cross is the length of the straight line segment between the two points.

The side length of the box is 1m, so the highlighted right-angled triangle has base length 2m and height 1m. By Pythagoras' theorum, the resulting distance between the two points is $\sqrt{2^2 + 1^2}$m$=\sqrt{5}$m $= 2.236$

**154** 720° for all. Even for a football (20 hexagons and 12 pentagons) the deficit is 720°. This is an illustration of a remarkable theorem of Gauss, which says that the solid angle subtended at a point inside any simply-closed figure is equal to $4\pi$, or 720°. This is the case for a sphere where by definition, the solid angle at the centre is $4\pi$. For the platonic solids, all the curvature resides exclusively in the vertices and is equal to the sum of the angular deficit at the vertices.

**155** 5 per cent.

The annual rise in price of anything is a compound multiplier. The way to think about the effect of a price rise of $x$ per cent over, say, two years is that if the price was originally P0 then the price P2 after two years will be $(1 + x\%) \times (1 + x\%) \times P0$.

So, if the price P6 is $1.333 \times P0$ after six years then we can find $x$ by solving $(1 + x\%)^6 = 1.333$. This is given by $x\% = (1.333)^{1/6} - 1$ = 5 per cent.

Although an annual price rise of 5 per cent is rather more than inflation, it is difficult to describe this as a jump in a single year, although of course it is significant when compounded over six years.

**156**  360° and 810°.

Smallest = 90 + 60 + 90 + 120.

The rhombus is a square, the isosceles triangle is equilateral, the biggest angle in a right–angled triangle is always 90 and the hexagon is regular.

Largest = 180 + 180 + 90 + 360.

The rhombus is long and thin, the isosceles triangle is very squat, the biggest angle in a right–angled triangle is always 90 and the hexagon is irregular with a 360 reflex internal angle.

**157**  One solution is:

$$\sqrt{\sqrt{8+8}}$$

because

$$\sqrt{\sqrt{8+8}}=\sqrt{\sqrt{16}}=\sqrt{4}= 2.$$

**158**  The next number in the sequence is intended to be 1. Reversing the order of digits we find the sequence: 16, 25, 36, 49, 64, 81. This is the sequence: $4^2, 5^2, 6^2, 7^2, 8^2, 9^2$. The next term in this sequence is $10^2 = 100$. Reversing digits, we find the number 001.

## 159 91.

Your journey will consist of going north 59 − 47 = 12 times and east 7 − 5 = 2 times. Each route can therefore be uniquely identified with a 14-letter string containing twelve Ns and two Es, and each such string corresponds to a route. An example journey could be NEENNNNNNNNNNN. This means you walk north at the first intersection, then east at the next two intersections, and walk directly north through the next 11 intersections to your final destination.

We can count all such 14-letter strings by noting that there are 14 choices of where to place the first E, and a remaining 13 choices for where to place the second E. However, this results in each journey being counted twice; placing the first E in position 2 and the second E in position 3 results in the same string as first E in position 3 and second E in position 2, etc.

The result is that we have (14 × 13)/2 = 91 such strings and so 91 journeys to the destination.

**160** Yes. Numbering the links from 1 to 63, Alex can remove links 5, 14 and 31. This produces three single removed links and four separate chains containing 4, 8, 16 and 32 links.

Since 63 = 32 + 16 + 8 + 4 + (1+1) + 1, you have the values of the columns in a six-digit binary number and so all numbers between 1 and 63 can be made up with a selection of them. Thus, on the $n^{th}$ day, Blair can, by suitable exchange with Alex, hold exactly $n$ links, leaving Alex with the remaining 63 − $n$ links. For example, on Day 12, Blair will be holding chains of lengths of 8 and 4 links (12 = 001100 in binary), and Alex will hold the others.

**161** Yes. We already know that Bill took the mango. Cathy and Drew don't like vanilla, so vanilla has to go to Athena, who is happy with that choice. The only fruit flavour left is strawberry, which goes to Drew. Cathy is left with chocolate, which she is happy with.

**162** One. Each egg gets two wrappers, so with two wrappers left, Bunny must have used 40, which means 20 eggs. Each egg gets different colours, so 19 eggs must have red on them. Therefore the other egg must be the only one with green and yellow wrappers.

**163** Yes. But life is difficult for Andy, because there's only one way to set the table that will keep everyone happy!

From (1) Andy can only sit next to Catherine and Danny. Since he must sit next to two people on a circular table, these are them, so Catherine – Andy – Danny must be sitting in this order (or in reverse order, depending how you like to count).

Catherine cannot sit next to Ellen by (4) or Ben by (3). The only option left is Fiona, so now we have the ordering Fiona – Catherine – Andy – Danny. By (2), Fiona can't sit next to Ellen, so Ben must go next to Fiona. The only place left now is between Ben and Danny, and the only person left is Ellen. Since she didn't argue with the boys, there is no problem with this arrangement. So, the solution for a circular table is: Ellen – Ben – Fiona – Catherine – Andy – Danny.

**164** 1 in 3 (33 per cent). The probability that John will turn his pancake over is one out of two possibilities, i.e. 50 per cent. The probability that Martha will turn her pancake over is two out of three possibilities, i.e. 67 per cent. So, the probability that they will both turn their pancakes over is 50 per cent × 67 per cent = 33 per cent (or more accurately 1/3).

**165** He should pour the milk in before the interview to reduce the rate of cooling over the next ten minutes.

**166** £3. You can set up a simple simultaneous equation where R = rum cocktail and C = carrot juice:

3R + 2C = 18

2R + 2C = 14

Subtracting these leaves you with R = 4, so C must be 3.

**167** Potatoes are the connection! Sir Walter Raleigh is widely thought to be responsible for introducing the potato to Europe. (Note that some modern historians dispute this claim.) The clues are King Edward (V), Vivaldi and Charlotte, which are three varieties of potato.

**168** Yes. The ratio of volumes of the top 4in, top 8in and whole cone is 1 cubed to 2 cubed to 3 cubed, i.e. 1:8:27, since they are similar figures, and volume scales as the cube of linear dimensions.

So Nick's middle section is 7/27 of the total amount of sugar, that is 7/20 of what was left for the other presenters. Since 7/20 is greater than 7/21 = 1/3, and each of the other presenters (those that got any) used 1/3 of what was left, Nick has more than enough sugar to sweeten his coffee.

**169**  30 glasses. If we suppose that the barrel contains $n$ glasses of wine, then on the second night each glass contains $(n–5)/n$ of the amount of alcohol that the glasses on the first night contained. You are equally tipsy on both nights, so we can work out that $5 = 6((n–5)/n)$ ➜ $5n = 6n–30$ ➜ $n = 30$.

**170**  Number 9. 13 is an unlucky number. Every natural number is divisible by 1 and itself. So, the sum of the divisors of a number is strictly greater than itself. This leaves 12 numbers to check. We find that 9 is the only number with the desired property. In particular, nine's divisors are 1, 3, 9, and $1 + 3 + 9 = 13$.

**171**  190ml. Justin has finished 90 per cent of his coffee when Sarah finishes hers. So, he drinks at 9/10 of her speed. In the same way, John drinks at 9/10 the speed of Justin. So John drinks at $(9/10) \times (9/10) = 81/100$ the speed of Sarah. So when Sarah finishes her litre, John is 81 per cent of the way there, with 190ml to go.

**172** Open the box that is labelled 'Apples and Oranges'. You know that since none of the labels are correct, the box must either contain only apples or only oranges. If you take an apple from that box, it must be the 'Apples Only' box. One of the two remaining boxes must be the 'Oranges Only' box. However, one is labelled 'Apples Only' and the other is labelled 'Oranges Only'. Therefore, the one labelled 'Apples Only' is the box that contains only oranges, and the box labelled 'Oranges Only' is the box that contains both kinds of fruit.

**173** Yes. Suppose that the relationship A ←→ B means that A and B know each other, for example. We can express the situation where each person knows exactly two other people as:

A ←→ B ←→ C ←→ D ←→ E ←→ F ←→ G ←→ H ←→ A.

From here you can see there are many solutions. Here are two, reading clockwise around the table:

A F D G B E H C A

A D F C E H B G A

**174**   Salmon = £2, cod = £5 and tuna = £7.

Monday: 10 salmon + 12 cod + 10 tuna = £150

Tuesday: 6 salmon + 15 cod + 9 tuna = £150

Wednesday: 23 salmon + 4 cod + 12 tuna = £150

There are several ways to solve this. Here's one.

If the stall sold *three* times as much as Wednesday this would be: 69 salmon + 12 cod + 36 tuna = £450

Compare to Monday: 69 salmon + 12 cod + 36 tuna − 10 salmon − 12 cod − 10 tuna = £450 − £150. So, 59 salmon + 26 tuna = £300

If he'd sold *five* times as much on Monday and *four* times as much on Tuesday this would be Monday: 50 salmon + 60 cod + 50 tuna = £750 and Tuesday: 24 salmon + 60 cod + 36 tuna = £600.

Comparing these, we can say that: 50 salmon + 60 cod + 50 tuna − 24 salmon − 60 cod − 36 tuna = £750 - £600 = £150.

So, 26 salmon + 14 tuna = £150. Double this is 52 salmon + 28 tuna = £300.

This means that 59 salmon + 26 tuna = 52 salmon + 28 tuna, i.e. 7 salmon = 2 tuna.

Multiply this by 13 and we get 91 salmon = 26 tuna.

We know that 59 salmon + 26 tuna = £300, so 59 salmon + 91 salmon = £300, which means 150 salmon = £300.

So, the price of salmon is £2 per portion. 7 salmon is £14.

7 salmon = 2 tuna, which is £14, so tuna is £7 per portion.

Looking at Monday's takings, 10 salmon + 12 cod + 10 tuna = £150, i.e. £20 + 12 cod + £70 = 150.

12 cod + £90 = £150, so 12 cod = £60, i.e. cod = £5 per portion.

**175** The number of pieces of chocolate increases by one with each break.

Starting with the single 3 × 8 piece of chocolate, we see that 23 breaks are needed to finish with the 24 squares of chocolate.

**176** 35 minutes. The smaller one has diameter d, so the bigger one has diameter $2^{1/3}$d. Time for the first is one hour, so time for the second is therefore $2^{2/3}$ hours = 1.59 hours, that is, 35 minutes longer.

**177**  400 BLUE, 320 SILVER and 1,280 GOLD.

The proportions are the same each year, so we can consider what these proportions are by comparing one year to the next. Look at each tier in turn:

BLUE: This tier will consist of existing BLUE members who stay in the BLUE tier and existing SILVER and GOLD members who move to the BLUE tier. This is equal to one-fifth of all members (i.e. next year's blue tier will consist wholly of this year's customers who earned less than 1,000 points). One-fifth of all members: one-fifth of 2,000 = 400.

SILVER: Existing BLUE members can move to SILVER if they earn the points, but existing SILVER members will either move down to BLUE or up to GOLD. Existing GOLD members either stay in GOLD or move to BLUE. So next year's SILVER members will only consist of those BLUE members who earned at least 1,000 points, i.e. four-fifths of the BLUE members, four-fifths of 400 = 320.

GOLD: Existing BLUE members can't move to GOLD next year; they can only go up one tier in any one year. Existing SILVER members can move to GOLD if they earn their points and existing GOLD members can remain in GOLD if they earn their points. So next year's GOLD members will consist of four-fifths of this year's SILVER and four-fifths of this year's GOLD members.

Write this as the equation GOLD = 4/5 × SILVER + 4/5 × GOLD
Rearrange to: 1/5 GOLD = 4/5 SILVER
Which gives 1/5 GOLD = 4/5 × 320 = 256
So GOLD = 256 × 5 = 1,280.

We can verify all this by noting that BLUE + SILVER + GOLD = 400 + 320 + 1280 = 2,000 which is the total number of customers.

**178** 66.5° (approximately). This is best seen by drawing a diagram in which Earth is an inclined circle, with its axis tilted away from the sun's rays. With the Earth rotated over by 23.5°, then the complement of this angle is the latitude at the top. In short, 90° − 23.5° = 66.5°.

**179** Seven trips. Take the ptarmigan over. Return. Take the polar willow over. Return with the ptarmigan. Take the Arctic fox over. Return. Take the ptarmigan over. So, there are seven crossings — four forward and three back, and no specimens are eaten in the process.

**180** 24,837 miles.

If Thule is 16 when they set off, then Suvi is 2.5 times this age = 40. When they return, Suvi is twice the age of Thule.

If they take Y years to go around the world, from pole to pole and back again, then Suvi is 40 + Y years old and Thule is 16 + Y years old. So Suvi's age = 40 + Y = twice Thule's age = 2 (16 + Y). Solving this equation gives Y = 8 years.

We are finally told that they travel at 8.5 miles per day. Eight years is 2,922 days (not forgetting the two leap days), so travelling at this speed means that they covered a total of 8.5 × 2,922 = 24,837 miles.

**181** One minute.

The quickest way over the river is straight across. In order to do that, the bear must swim at an angle into the current. With the resultant velocity towards the reporter being straight across the fjord, and the current flow at right angles to the banks, one can use Pythagoras' theorem (adjacent length squared + opposite length squared = hypotenuse length squared) to find the size of the resultant velocity.

Here the hypotenuse is 10km/h (relative to the surface, the bear always swims at 10km/h), and the opposite velocity is the current, given by 8km/h, making the adjacent velocity towards the reporter 6km/h. This means the bear could swim 1km in ten minutes, and thus 100m in one minute.

For clarity, while the bear's velocity is realistic, the current velocity has a high chance of being possible.

**182** 50 per cent. Since we are dealing with proportions, we don't need to know the initial amount. 100 per cent minus 1.7 per cent is how much mass is reduced from one year to the next. Keep multiplying the resultant amount by this proportion 40 times to find the total reduction. Or you can write is as an equation: $(100\%-1.7\%)^{40}$ equals (pretty much) 50 per cent.

**183**  10cm: Use the 50cm bit and then pour in 40cm of water
$(50 - 40 = 10)$

20cm: Use the 30cm bit twice and pour in 40cm of water
$(2 \times 30 - 40 = 20)$

30cm:  $30 = 30$
40cm:  $30 + 50 - 40 = 40$
50cm:  $50 = 50$
60cm:  $2 \times 30 = 60$
70cm:  $2 \times 30 + 50 - 40 = 70$
80cm:  $30 + 50 = 80$
90cm:  $3 \times 30 = 90$
100cm: $2 \times 50 = 100$

**184**  They all won a third consecutive European Cup/Champions League title in the years shown.

**185**  £0.50. This is similar to a famous 'bat and ball' problem set by Nobel Prize-winning economist Daniel Kahneman, in which 50 per cent of Harvard, MIT and Princeton students gave the intuitive – but incorrect – answer. In our question, you may have been tempted to say the bottle of water costs £1. However, if this were the case, the souvenir t-shirt would cost £11 (£10 more), which would make a total of £12. The correct answer is that the bottle of water is £0.50 and souvenir t-shirt is £10.50.

**186** The first letters of the names of the stadia for each football club spell out the word 'LEFT' to honour the left-handers day. London Stadium (West Ham), Etihad Stadium (Manchester City), Fratton Park (Portsmouth), Turf Moor (Burnley).

**187** Bruno and Shirley give 6 points each and Craig gives 3. As the average score is 6, the total score by the four judges is 24. Darcey has given 9, so the remaining three judges give a score of 15 between them. 6 + 6 + 3 = 15.

**188** 30km/h. The first half (60km distance at 60km/h) was completed in one hour and the second part (60km distance at 20km/h) was completed in three hours. The average speed is *not* the average of the speeds, but rather it is the total distance divided by the total time: 120km/4 hours = 30km/h.

**189** 80km/h. When the spot is at its highest point, because the centre of the wheel is going at 40km/h, the bottom of the wheel is stationary (in contact with the road) so the top of the wheel must be going at twice the speed of the bike.

**190** 32. For the first of Germany's penalties there are two possible outcomes: score (S) or miss (M). For the first two there are $2 \times 2 = 2^2 = 4$ possible outcomes: SS, SM, MS and MM. For all five before the sudden death phase, there are $2^5 = 32$ possible outcomes (e.g. MSMMS).

**191** The son's weight is insufficient to melt the ice so there is no liquid film on the underside of the skate to help it move along.

**192** 14. This can be achieved by placing eight bishops along the bottom row of the board and six across the six non-corner squares of the top row.

To see why 15 (or more) bishops can't be placed on the board with no two attacking each, we can observe that there are exactly 15 diagonals covering the board from south-east to north-west:

$$a1 - a1, \quad b1 - a2, \quad c1 - a3, \quad d1 - a4, \quad e1 - a5, \quad f1 - a6, \quad g1 - a7,$$
$$h1 - a8, \quad h2 - b8, \quad h3 - c8, \quad h4 - d8, \quad h5 - e8, \quad h6 - f8,$$
$$h7 - g8, \quad h8 - h8.$$

We can put at most one bishop on each of these diagonals, because any two bishops on the same diagonal attack one another. So, we cannot put more than 15 bishops on a board with no two attacking each other.

Finally, the $a1 - a1$ and $h8 - h8$ diagonals of length 1 sit on the same south-west to north-east diagonal, so only one of the $a1 - a1$, $h8 - h8$ diagonals can be occupied, which means that at most 14 of the south-east to north-west diagonals can contain a bishop.

**193**  163. This puzzle is all about the spacing between triples. There is always a gap of two. But the bull becomes useful at 170, so that one of the gaps between triples disappears. Then another bull comes into play at 160, so that below 160 there is always a combination of t20 and 50 that fills in the space between adjacent triples.

180 = t20 + t20 + t20
179 gap
178 gap
177 = t20 + t20 + t19
166 gap
165 gap
174 = t20 + t20 + t18
173 gap
172 gap
171 = t20 + t20 + t17
170 = t20 + t20 + 50 in creeps the bull
169 gap
168 = t20 + t20 + t16
167 = t20 + 50 + t19
166 gap
165 = t20 + t20 + t15
164 = t20 + 50 + t18
163 gap
162 = t20 + t20 + t14
161 = t20 + 50 + t17
160 =  50 + 50 + t20 another bull can be used
159 = t20 + t20 + t13

158 = t20 + 50 + t16
157 = 50 + 50 + t19
There are 9 impossible scores: 63   166   169   172   173   175
176   178   179.

**194** No, it requires four lines. The two white corners are start/end points, but the edge squares are stranded unless the line from corner to corner goes through them. This covers 14 white squares and effectively reduces the problem to a new one with a 6 × 6 chess board. The same procedure with a new line reduces the board to 4 × 4. A third line gives a 2 × 2 board. The final two squares are then covered by a fourth line.

**195** Six. This may be easier to see with a real football in front of you. Place the first red face on the ground. The 19 remaining white faces can be arranged by ascending height, in layers containing three, six, six, three and one face, respectively. In either of the layers of three, whichever of the three faces I choose, the result looks the same, because I can rotate through 120° about a vertical axis. I could paint the single face at the top. From the higher layer of six, there are two essentially different choices, but all choices from the lower layer of six produce the same result – as can be seen by rotating about a neighbouring black pentagonal face as well.

**196** Backwards, according to Newton's first law. It may skid though!

**197** 99.7 per cent (i.e. it's virtually certain this will happen!). The chance of them all being different is determined as follows:

The second bicycle sold must be different to the first (i.e. one of the remaining 39) and the third must be different again (i.e. one of the remaining 38), and so on until we consider the twentieth bicycle sold, which must be different to the other 19 (i.e. one of the remaining 21).

Multiply all this together and we get:
$(39/40) \times (38/40) \times (37/40) \times \ldots \times (21/40) = 0.0031$.

So the chances of at least two being the same is $1 - 0.0031 = 0.9969$: i.e. 99.7 per cent.

**198** 23 games. In a pure knockout system, the first round would consist of 12 games, the next round 6 games, the next round 3.

At this point, 3 teams remain, so one team goes straight to the final and the other two teams play off (game 22) before the final (game 23.)

The quickest way to reach this result is that in a 24-team tournament, 23 teams have to lose, so 23 games is the bare minimum.

**199** 14,336. Say England is in Group G. The matches in the group stage are already determined, so there is no choice there. In the first match of the knockout round (final 16) they could play any of the four teams in Group H. In their quarter-final they could play any of the eight teams in Groups E and F. In their semi-final they could play any of the 16 teams in Groups A, B, C and D.

In the final, they could play the other team from Group G that got through (three possibilities), any of the three teams in Group H that they didn't already play, any of the seven teams in E and F they didn't already play, or any of the 15 teams in A, B, C and D that they didn't already play.

The total number of possibilities is therefore $4 \times 8 \times 16 \times (3 + 3 + 7 + 15) = 14{,}336$.

**200** 380. There are multiple methods to solve this. In brief, every team faces 19 other teams twice a season (home and away). This is $19 \times 2 = 38$. So the total number of matches is the sum of the sequence $38 + 36 + 34 + \dots + 6 + 4 + 2$. This is the same mathematically as $2 \times (19)(20)/2 = 380$.

**201**   34. The number of seven punch combos is the same as the number of seven letter sequences of $J$ and $U$ with no $U$ followed by a consecutive $U$. We'll call a sequence of $J$ and $U$ 'punchable' if the sequence contains no two consecutive $U$s and count the number of punch combinations by counting the number of punchable sequences.

Every punchable sequence starts with a $J$ or a $U$, and we will count the number of punchable sequences by adding the number of punchable sequences starting with $J$ and starting with $U$.

There are the same number of punchable sequences of length $n$ as there are punchable sequences of length $n + 1$ which start with a $J$ (the $J$ can be added/dropped to give the correspondence).

We can't have consecutive $U$s, so any punchable sequence of length $n + 1$ which starts with a $U$ must have second letter $J$. This means the total number of punchable sequences of length $n + 1$ starting with a $U$ corresponds to the number of punchable sequences of length $n - 1$ which make up the remaining $n - 1$ letters which follow $U, J$.

We can conclude that:
#(punchable length $n + 1$) = #(punchable length $n$)+
#(punchable length $n - 1$):

There are two punchable sequences of length 1 and three of length 2.

It follows that the number of punchable sequence of length $n$ is the $(n + 2)$nd Fibonacci number.

So, the number of seven punch combos the boxer can throw is 34.

**202** There are 21 possible orders that the goals could have been scored in, listed below.

Those with a mathematical background will recognise this result as 7C2 or '7 choose 2', i.e. the number of ways of choosing two items from seven items. In this case, the two items are Japanese goals, and the 7 items are any goals in the game.

UUUUUJJ
UUUUJJU (this is what actually happened)
UUUUJUJ
UUUJJUU
UUUJUJU
UUUJUUJ
UUJJUUU
UUJUJUU
UUJUUJU
UUJUUUJ
UJJUUUU
UJUJUUU
UJUUJUU
UJUUUJU
UJUUUUJ
JJUUUUU
JUJUUUU
JUUJUUU
JUUUJUU
JUUUUJU
JUUUUUJ

**203** Betting is bad for you, and in this case bad for John. The probability of him winning this bet is 1 in 3 (or about 33.33 per cent). The reason is counter-intuitive: because we read the results of coin tosses in order, we don't flip a coin three times, see the results, and then if nobody wins flip the coin three more times (this would have been a fair game).

If the first two tosses are heads, then automatically John will lose. Even if the coin keeps bringing heads for many more tosses, eventually tails will come up and at that moment Mishal wins, since the last two throws will have been heads.

On the other hand, if the first two tosses are heads–tails, John won't necessarily win, as the third one might be tails again. So the whole betting restarts with toss number four, as tails–tails doesn't work for any player.

Moreover, if the first two tosses are either tails–tails or tails–heads, no player gets an advantage over the other. In other words, Mishal wins more often than John.

In symbols, if you let p be the probability that Mishal wins, the description above gives the equation: $p = 1/4 + p/8 + p/2$ and so $p = 2/3$.

**204** Four times.

First we need to work out when they pass each other for the first time. At the point they meet, they have been travelling for the same amount of time (T). The distance covered by Mishal in the red cart is 20T. The distance covered by Nick in the blue one is 30T. We know the circumference of the track is 60km, so $60 = 20T + 30T = 50T$. Which means that $T = 6/5$ hours, i.e. they meet after an hour and 12 minutes.

After passing on the track, it takes them exactly one hour and 12 minutes to meet again. So, it will be six hours before they meet at the starting point. Both carts need to do full circles. The red does a full circle every two hours (2, 4, 6) and the blue one every three hours (3, 6) so the earliest they can meet at the starting point is at six hours.

Knowing that they passed each other every hour and 12 minutes at some point around the circle means that after six hours had passed, they had met five times. The answer to the question is four, not five, because the question excludes the meeting at the starting point, which happens at six hours.

**205** She can if she was listening carefully.

1. From John's first line, the novelist knows that a blonde woman has a cat, and another woman has a snake.

2. From Martha's line, someone with a ponytail has at least one dog.

3. From John's second line, a man with blue hair had trouble walking two pets.

4. The novelist witnesses that of the three people involved, one had a shaved head.

From the initial description in the puzzle, there are two girls and a boy. From John's first line, the boy cannot have a cat or a snake, so Martha is talking about the man with a ponytail. Therefore, the man in statements 2) and 3) above is the same person! So he has blue hair with a ponytail and two pets, one of which is a dog. From 1), the cat owner is a blonde woman. And from 1) and 4) together the snake is owned by a woman with a shaved head. The only pet remaining is the second dog, so it has to belong to the man.

**206** 18.67km.

At the point Martha's train overtakes Nick's, they have both travelled the same distance; the difficulty comes from their different start times. Assume the trains met $T$ hours after 10:12. Nick's slow train travelled $55T$ km. The fast train started 12 minutes later (1/5 of an hour). Travelling for $T - 0.2$ hours it covered distance $70(T - 0.2)$ km.

Since the distances are the same when they meet, we can write it as the equation $70(T - 0.2) = 55T$, or $15T = 14$. This gives us $T = 14/15$ hours, or 56 minutes.

So, the trains pass at 11:08 at a distance of 51.33km from their starting point. This makes it 18.67km from Brighton.

**207** 55. There are eight words ending end in 's', not counting the 's' itself or the three occurrences of 'is'. So, that's eight places for a right or wrong. But we're also told that he doesn't get two rights in a row. There is one way to get them all wrong. There are eight ways to get exactly one right. There are 21 ways to get exactly two right. There are 20 ways to get exactly three right. Lastly, there are five ways to get exactly four right. It is impossible to get five or more right. $1 + 8 + 21 + 20 + 5 = 55$.

**208** Part 1: There are definitely a few ways to separate the balls into boxes so that the trick works. One such way would be to put balls 1–5 in Box 1, 6–10 in Box 2 and so on, until finally all balls with numbers larger than 30 are in the last box, Box 7. That way, Justin would very quickly be able to work out which box Mishal selected the balls from. For instance, if the sum was 15, she must have selected Box 1. If the sum is 40, then she selected Box 2, and so on. Can you find more ways?

Part 2: This solution can be a bit tricky because it requires you to remember that any number divided by 7 (we have seven boxes) has a remainder of 0, 1, 2, ... 6. For example:

$87 = 84 + 3 = 7 \times 12 + 3$, so it has remainder 3.
$140 = 20 \times 7 + 0$, so it has remainder 0 (or in other words, it is divided perfectly by 7).

We split the 200 balls as follows:

Box 1: Remainder 0 (numbers that divide perfectly by seven: 7, 14, 21...)
Box 2: Remainder 1: 1, 8, 15, 22...
Box 3: Remainder 2: 2, 9, 16, 23...
Keep going until ...
Box 7: Remainder 6: 6, 13, 20, 27...

And now, the real essence of the trick. Suppose that Mishal picks five balls from Box 6. Each of those numbers has a remainder 5 from the way Justin separated the balls. Adding numbers means we also add remainders, so after the addition, the total remainder is
$5 + 5 + 5 + 5 + 5 = 25$, which in turn has remainder 4 when divided by 7.

No matter which balls are selected from Box 6, their sum will always leave remainder 4 when divided by 7.

Moreover, repeating the procedure for all boxes gives different remainders for each box number. So all Justin needs to do is divide by 7, check the remainder and identify the box.

The solution is then given by:

1)    Remainder of sum is 0 means balls came from BOX 1

2)    Remainder of sum is 1 means balls came from BOX 4

3)    Remainder of sum is 2 means balls came from BOX 7

4)    Remainder of sum is 3 means balls came from BOX 3

5)    Remainder of sum is 4 means balls came from BOX 6

6)    Remainder of sum is 5 means balls came from BOX 2

7)    Remainder of sum is 6 means balls came from BOX 5

**209** The first train from Edinburgh arrives into London at 12:30. So, departing at 12:00 from London, Mishal passes every train that departs Edinburgh before she arrives in Edinburgh at 18:00, which are the 12 trains that departed from Edinburgh between 06:30 and 17:30.

**210** Nine. An arrangement in which no-one gets the right coffee is called a 'derrangement'. There are 24 possible arrangements of four objects; by listing them all and crossing off those where one is in its right place, it can be seen that there are nine derrangements of four objects.

**211** With a cut that spirals as it goes around the bagel. This cuts it into two pieces that are linked and therefore cannot be shared.

**212** Duncan. The tapes are being read in the wrong horizontal direction, meaning that the binary for each letter is reversed. Under this transformation, the only letters that stay the same are 'D', 'J', 'N', 'Q', 'U'. So the name has six letters with 1st, 2nd, 3rd and 6th from that list. The only answer (according to the name lists we've searched) is 'Duncan'.

**213** John Humphrys.

If Justin is right that Mishal is wrong, then Mishal's claim that Justin is right is incorrect. This means Justin can't be right.

If Mishal is right, then her claim that Justin is right means his claim that Mishal is wrong is correct. This means Mishal can't be right.

Finally, John's claim does not contain a contradiction, so he must be right. But the quick answer is that John Humphreys is always right!

**214** Justin should ask a completely innocuous question (effectively, waste his turn). If he did manage to reduce John, for example, to a gibbering wreck then Martha would ask Justin an incisive question with a two-thirds chance of it succeeding. But if Justin wastes his turn, either Martha knocks out John or John knocks out Martha and Justin then gets a chance at the remaining person. It's still not a great chance, but better than the alternative.

**215** Six. This type of braid is known as a 'Brunnian braid' and is similar to the 'Borromean Rings'. The braid consists of three topological circles that are linked in at least 6 places, but where removing any one ring leaves the other two unconnected.

**216** Justin, Martha and Mishal conspired against Nick and ate the cake without him! We know that at least one of the presenters ate some cake. There are three cases:

Case 1: If Justin ate some cake then Mishal's testimony would implicate Martha. From
Justin's testimony, if Martha ate some cake then so did Mishal.

Case 2: If Martha ate some cake then, according to Justin's statement, so did Mishal. From
Martha's statement we know that Justin ate some if Mishal did.

Case 3: If Mishal ate some cake, then Martha's testimony must mean that Justin ate some.
But if Justin ate some cake then so did Martha according to Mishal!

In all three cases, if one of the presenters ate some cake then all three presenters ate some.

As we know that at least one presenter ate some cake, we can conclude that all three presenters ate all the cake without Nick.

**217** Approximately 3.6m.

The ball will bounce off the front wall on the way to Justin. The journey the ball takes from the front wall to Justin is the same length as the journey it would take from the front wall to Justin if he was standing in the mirror position on the other side of the front wall.

Putting Justin in his new position, which is 3m from where the front wall used to be, the ball travels 5m in a straight line after John hits it. We can form a right-angled triangle using John, Justin and his side wall. This triangle has hypotenuse of length 5m (the distance the ball travels), and the side along the wall has length 4m (3m into the new room plus John's distance of 1m from the wall). Pythagoras' theorem tells us John is standing 3m from Justin's side wall.

Putting Justin back to his original position, we see a new right-angled triangle formed between John, Justin and his side wall, with legs of lengths 3m (John's distance to Justin's side wall) and 2m (Justin's distance to the front wall minus John's distance). The distance between John and Justin is the length of the hypotenuse of this triangle. Pythagoras' theorem tells us that the distance between John and Justin is the square root of $3^2 + 2^2 = 13$, which is approximately 3.6m.

**218**  357.

John is allowed to eat the chocolates labelled 5, 10, 15 up to 500. Since 500 = 5(100), John is allowed to eat 100 chocolates.

Mishal is allowed to eat the chocolates labelled 7, 14, 21 up to 497. Since 497 = 7(71), Mishal is allowed to eat 71 chocolates.

They agree to leave the chocolates labelled with multiples of the lowest common multiple of 5 and 7, which is 35. That is, the arithmetic sequence 35, 70, 105 and so on up to 490. Since 490 = 35(14), there are 14 chocolates which they won't eat from their own allowance.

So, John eats 100 − 14 = 86 sweets and Mishal eats 71 − 14 = 57 sweets.

500 − (86 + 57) = 357 sweets left uneaten.

**219**  2.5mph. At 10mph the 15-mile ride takes Martha 1.5 hours, and she waits that time again so John has taken three hours. He got his puncture after one hour, so he walks the remaining five miles in two hours, which is 2.5 mph.

**220**  Five. There are $N$ jars and one is half full, so the amount of jam (in units of jars) is $N − 0.5$. If they are all filled to amount $x$ jars, then $N − 0.5 = Nx$. This gives $N = 0.5/(1 − x)$. We have $x = 0.9$ so $N = 5$.

**221** 8.43 and 38 seconds. The hands on a conventional clock coincide 11 times in 12 hours, so each crossing is 12/11 of an hour apart. The eighth crossing is at 8 × (12/11) = 8.7272 hours, or 8:43:38.

**222** Imagine that rope 1 is A–B and rope 2 is C–D. Light ends A, B and C simultaneously. When rope 1 is burnt out (that's 20 minutes), light end D. When rope 2 is burnt out that's 30 minutes.

**223** Three. For example, she might use yellow on top, red, blue, red, blue around the four sides and yellow on the bottom.

**224** One-third of it, or 209cm. Suppose the tree is a cylinder centred at O, radius R and Martha is at M. Its circumference is 628cm so its radius is 100cm. This means that Martha is a distance R from the surface of the cylinder. The tangent to the cylinder from M is at T, and the angle MOT is 60°. This means that Martha can see 120° of the tape, which is one-third or 209cm.

**225** 4,189cm³. The fact that the diameters of the hole or the melon are not given means that the answer doesn't depend on these. So, let the hole diameter be zero so that the length of the hole is then the diameter of the melon. The volume of a sphere of radius 10cm is 4,189cm³. It is possible to prove that the remaining volume is indeed independent of the hole and sphere diameters.

**226** There are three alternative ways of buying toffees and trees for £200:

1. 20 bags of toffees
2. 13 bags of toffees and 2 trees
3. 6 bags of toffees and 4 trees.

If $X$ = the number of toffees and $Y$ = the number of trees, then $10X + 35Y = 200$

Re-write this equation as: $X = (200 - 35Y)/10 = 20 - 3Y - (5Y/10)$

Let $P = (5Y/10)$
So $2P = Y$ and $X = 20 - 7P$

| P | Y trees | X toffees |
|---|---------|-----------|
| 0 | 0 | 20 |
| 1 | 2 | 13 |
| 2 | 4 | 6 |

**227** 60°. When the chain is pulled hard at one point, B, then the chain BAB follows the line of shortest length, a geodesic (assuming no friction and a light flexible chain). The midpoint A is the highest point.

If you unwrap the cone so that it is flat, then the shortest distance BAB is a straight line. For the line to pass over the vertex V, then the angle V must increase until the unwrapped cone becomes a semicircle (the limiting case). Then A coincides with V and the line BAB (which is the same as BVB) lies along the diameter.

If the radius of this semicircle is R, then the base circumference of the cone is πR so that the base diameter is R. The side view of the cone is therefore an equilateral triangle, which makes the cone angle 60°.

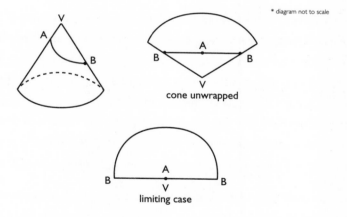

\* diagram not to scale

cone unwrapped

limiting case

**228** Eight times more. The volume of a three-dimensional object goes as the cube of its size. So, a sphere, a cube, a cone of twice the size has eight times the volume.

**229** The gold star. We know from the last sentence that Nick got John's gift, and John and Justin did not get anything from Mishal or Martha. So, it must be that John got either Nick's gift or Justin's. Suppose for a moment that John got Nicks's Santa. Then, since Justin did not get anything from the ladies and since Nick and John got each other's gifts, it must be that Justin ended up with his own gift, which we know did not happen. So our assumption that John got the Santa must be wrong and we know that John got Justin's angel. Then the only possibility for Justin's gift is the Santa. For the same reason, we now know that Mishal and Martha ended up with each other's ornaments, and therefore Mishal got the gold star.

**230** 808. The trick is to think about how many times each part appears. For example, the partridge is mentioned 12 times (counting up from one, then one and two, then one and two and three, etc. until we reach the full set of all 12 verses), so it's 12 times the number of legs in one mention. Likewise, for the turtle doves, they are mentioned a total of 11 times, and each time we have four legs, giving a total of 44. The number of times each verse is mentioned just counts down 12, 11, 10, 9, 8, etc. until we reach the final verse, with 12 drummers which is only mentioned once.

The only really tricky verse is eight maids a-milking, since we have eight maids = 16 legs, plus eight cows = 32 legs, giving 48 legs per mention. It's then mentioned in five verses so 5 × 48 = 240.

1 Partridge: 12 mentions × 2 legs each time = 24
2 Turtle doves: 11 mentions × 4 legs each time = 44

3 French hens: 10 mentions × 6 legs each time = 60

4 Calling birds: 9 mentions × 8 legs each time = 72

5 Rings: 8 mentions × 0 legs each time = 0

6 Geese: 7 mentions × 12 legs each time = 84

7 Swans: 6 mentions × 14 legs each time = 84

8 Maids + cows: 5 mentions x 48 legs each time = 240

9 Ladies: 4 mentions × 18 legs each time = 72

10 Lords: 3 mentions × 20 legs each time = 60

11 Pipers: 2 mentions × 22 legs each time = 44

12 Drummers: 1 mention × 24 legs each time = 24

**231** Andrew gets the jumper in the blue box. Bill gets the books in the red box. Cathy gets the green box with the robot.

We know that the presents are robot, books and jumper, and that the colours are red, blue and green. We are told that Cathy doesn't get the red present, so she must be either blue or green. We also know that the red box contains the books. We are also told that Andrew gets the blue present, which isn't the robot.

Since books are in the red box, the robot must be in either the blue or the green, but we know it's not in the blue, so the green box contains the robot. This leaves the sweater in the blue box that goes to Andrew. Because Cathy is not getting the red box with the books, we know this goes to Bill. So the green one with the robot goes to Cathy.

**232** Eight. Taking the first number as the height and the second as the width, we have the following possibilities: $1 \times 24, 2 \times 12, 3 \times 8, 4 \times 6,$ $6 \times 4, 8 \times 3, 12 \times 2, 24 \times 1$. This gives a total of eight different rectangles.

**233** No he is not! There are definitely 11 children coming, and there are only 16 chairs. The fastest way to see the solution is to start arranging the table by child-child-chair, child-child-chair, etc. It's possible to argue that with this method, the most number of children can sit around the table. Using this trick, you can see that up to seat number 15, you can fit $5 \times 2 = 10$ children at most. Since 11 children are definitely coming, they won't fit.

**234** 66,795. For the first 12 days one can fairly easily add $1 + 2 + 3 + \ldots + 12$ to find that 78 presents would be needed. Doing the same for 365 days is tiresome. This is an algebraic series, so the sum of the number of presents over n days is given by $n(a1 + an)/2$ where $a1$ is the number of presents on the first day (1), and $an$ is the number of presents on the $n$th day (n). With $n = 365$, the number of presents is 66,795. Good luck John!

**235** 99. The trick is based on special properties of numbers with a double digit. In this case, the potential number of elves is YY, where Y is a number from 1 to 9. This means that the number of elves (X) can be written as:

$$X = Y + 10Y$$

Now let's do the operations that Santa asks, keeping X as an unknown.

We have:

1. Multiply by 100:
$$100Y + 1000Y \text{ (number is YY00)}$$

2. Add 33:
$$1000Y + 100Y + 10 \times 3 + 3 = Y(1100) + 3 \times 11 \text{ (number is YY33)}$$

3. Divide by 11:
$$100Y + 3 \text{ (number is Y03)}$$

4. Add to the number the number in reverse:
$$(100Y + 3) + (3 \times 100 + Y) = 100(Y + 3) + (Y + 3)$$
$$= 101 \times (Y + 3)$$

6. Divide by 101: gies the final answer Y + 3.

Since Athena's final answer is 12, Y must be 9, and the number of elves must be 99!

You can make the trick more complicated if instead of 33, you add a random two-digit number with the same digit (e.g. 55 or 77). If you write your number as 10Z + Z, the result will always be Y + Z and you can find Y after that.

**236** About 21km.

The furthest distance from anywhere in the mainland UK to the Isle of Man is about 520km. The radius $R$ of the Earth is 6,371km. The triangle rule of Pythagoras says that if the height of the firework from the surface is $h$, then $(R + h)^2 = R^2 + ((R + h) \times \sin A)^2$, where A is the angle in radians from a line emanating from the centre of Earth to the Isle of Man and a line extending from the centre of the Earth a distance 520km from the Isle of Man (such as Folkestone).

Angle A is given by $520/R = 0.0818$ radians.

Assuming that the height of the firework will be significantly smaller than the radius of the Earth, we can simplify the Pythagoras equation to say $h = 0.5 \times R \times A^2$. Height $h$ is therefore about 21km – that's a pretty powerful firework!

**237** Six. 16 + 16 + 17 + 17 + 17 + 17 = 100.

**238** Yes.

He starts with 40 carrots. After 5,000 miles, he has used up five of them feeding the reindeer and four for carrying the four sacks, leaving 31 carrots. Note that he still needs four sacks to carry the 31 carrots.

After the next 5,000 miles, another five carrots have been used for feeding the reindeer and another four for carrying the sacks, leaving 22. Now there are only three sacks remaining that need to be carried.

For the next 5,000 miles, another five carrots are needed to feed the reindeer, but only three are used to carry the sacks, meaning a total of eight carrots are used up. There are now 14 carrots remaining in two sacks.

The next 5,000 miles require five carrots to feed the reindeer and two for the sacks, using up seven and leaving seven in one sack.

Santa can then travel the last 4,901 miles using five carrots to feed the reindeer and one to carry the final sack until the end. He therefore completes his journey with exactly 1 carrot remaining.

**239** Ten. The pattern is that lockers visited an even number of times will be closed at the end. For example, the 15th locker will be visited by elves whose numbers are factors of 15 (i.e. 1, 3, 5, 15). This represents four elves (an even number), which means the locker will, in turn, be: open, closed, open, closed.

Now all numbers with an even number of factors will end up closed. And all numbers, except perfect squares, have an even number of factors if we include 1 and the number itself. For a perfect square (say, 16) we have factors 1, 2, 4, 8 and 16 (an odd number of factors) and the lockers would be: open, closed, open, closed, open. We can conclude that all the lockers whose numbers are perfect squares will be open at the completion of the exercise. There are ten perfect squares between and including 1 and 100 (square root of 100 = 10), which are: 1, 4, 9, 16, 25, 36, 49, 64, 81 and 100. Therefore, those ten lockers will be open at the end of the process and the others closed.

**240** Santa took an erratic zigzagging route across the world and got lost many times. To account for the excessive distance travelled he had to travel at a significant fraction of the speed of light. Due to the time dilation phenomenon from special relativity, less time passed for Santa and the clock he took with him than it did on the ground at home. So, his turkey was left in the oven for longer than three hours.

**241** 27. For each of the three gifts, there are three choices for who should present it, if we allow each presenter to present more than one gift or none at all. $3 \times 3 \times 3 = 27$.

**242** The remaining part of the sequence is Venus, Saturn, Sol and the odd one out is Saturn.

It's a mythology puzzle with the sequence (at least in English) in Norse. Equivalence is less clear than with Roman/Greek deities. But thankfully, the romance languages use Roman deities.

Mani (moon deity = Luna, Lundi)
Tie (war = Mars, Mardi)
Oden (messenger to Hell, Mercury, Mercredi)
Thor (thunder, Jeudi, Jupiter)

So the remaining gods are:
Frigg (wisdom, love – less a direct relationship, but corresponding to Venus, Vendredi)
Saturn – the odd one out (time, but Roman not Norse, and doesn't correspond to a day because the romance languages use the day of the Sabbath)
Sunna (sun, Sol – again, romance languages call it day of the lord).

**243** Another five minutes. In five minutes, the temperature difference with the surroundings halved from 160 to 80 degrees Celsius. In another five minutes, it will halve again from 100 to 50 degrees Celsius.

**244** First, no L ('Noel') should definitely feel appropriate for the time of year. Second, L is the 12th letter of the alphabet, and there are 26 letters in the alphabet. 26/12 should make you think of Boxing Day.

**245** 75m. The four trees are equally spaced, so there are three gaps. Hence the distance is 3 × 25m.

**246** 9.5m of tinsel and 15 baubles.

The height and width of the tree goes as the cubed root of its weight. So, the height and width are 0.79 times those of last year's tree. The tinsel needs to cover the distance so 0.79 × 12 is 9.5m.

The surface area goes as height squared, so the area to decorate is 0.63 times that of last year. If the bauble decoration density (perhaps we can define this as 'tastefulness'!) is the same as last year, then the number of baubles goes down by the area, 0.63 × 24 = 15.

**247** 99.8 per cent. The chance of at least one flashing is the opposite of asking the chance that none at all are flashing. There are $8 \times 8 \times 8 = 512$ combinations, of which only one is steady/steady/steady. The chance of this is $1/512 = 0.2$ per cent. So, the chance of this not happening is $100 - 0.2 = 99.8$ per cent.

**248** The glass is twice as thick. The surface area of a sphere goes up as radius squared, so a bauble of twice the size ought to be four times heavier if the thickness is the same. So, the thickness must be doubled to double the weight up to eight.

**249** 176ml. One litre of alcohol-free mull contains 600ml of liquid. Suppose I add volume V ml of whisky at 40 per cent, then the alcohol content is 0.4V and the water content is 0.6V. The end product has an alcohol content expressed as a percentage of $100 \times 0.4V/(0.6V + 600)$ and this needs to be 10 per cent, so $40V = 6V + 6,000$, $34V = 6,000$ so $V = 6,000/34 = 176$ml.

**250** 2 in 11. Here are all the 11 possible selections for the four people in order A, B, C and D, noting that gift (1) doesn't appear in the first column and gifts (2) and (3) aren't in columns B and C:

| A | B | C | D |
|---|---|---|---|
| 2 | 1 | 4 | 3 |
| 2 | 3 | 1 | 4< |
| 2 | 3 | 4 | 1 |
| 2 | 4 | 1 | 3 |
| 3 | 1 | 2 | 4< |
| 3 | 1 | 4 | 2 |
| 3 | 4 | 1 | 2 |
| 3 | 4 | 2 | 1 |
| 4 | 1 | 2 | 3 |
| 4 | 3 | 1 | 2 |
| 4 | 3 | 2 | 1 |

Of these, Santa (column D) gets gift (4) in two of the 11 selection scenarios (marked <), hence the probability is 2/11.

This is tricky to generalise to larger groups. You might like to try! Here are the first few for groups of N people:

| N | probability |
|---|---|
| 2 | 0/1 |
| 3 | 1/3 |
| 4 | 2/11 |
| 5 | 9/53 |
| 6 | 44/309 |
| 7 | 265/2119 |
| 8 | 1854/16687 |
| 9 | 14833/148329 |

Is the limit as N gets very big equal to 1/N?

## 251 364.

Day 1: A partridge in a pear tree.
Day 2: Two turtle doves and a partridge in a pear tree.
Day 3: Three French hens, two turtle doves and a partridge in a pear tree, etc. up to 12 days.

So the answer is: One partridge on 12 days, two doves on 11 days, etc.

$= (1 \times 12) + (2 \times 11) + (3 \times 10) + (4 \times 9) + (5 \times 8) + (6 \times 7) \ldots$

$+ (7 \times 6) + (8 \times 5) + (9 \times 4) + (10 \times 3) + (11 \times 2) + (12 \times 1)$
$= 364$

# APPENDIX

# *Today* Presenters

**Jack de Manio** (1958–71)
**Robert Hudson** (1964–68)
**John Timpson** (1964, 1970–76, 1978–86)
**Robert Robinson** (1971–74)
**Barry Norman** (1974–76)
**Desmond Lynam** (1974–75)
**Paul Barnes** (1975–77)
**Brian Redhead** (1975–93)
**Gillian Reynolds** (1976)
**Nigel Rees** (1976–78)
**Libby Purves** (1978–81)
**Peter Hobday** (1983–96)
**Jenni Murray** (1985–87)
**Sue MacGregor** (1984–2002)
**Anna Ford** (1993–99)
**Andrew Marr** (2005–14)
**Edward Stourton** (1999–2009)
**Carolyn Quinn** (2004–08)
**Evan Davis** (2007–14)
**James Naughtie** (1994–2015)
**Sarah Montague** (2001–18)
**John Humphrys** (1987–2019)
**Justin Webb** (2009–)
**Mishal Husain** (2013–)
**Nick Robinson** (2015–)
**Martha Kearney** (2018–)

## NEWSREADERS

**Chris Aldridge**
**Corrie Corfield**
**Caroline Nicholls**
**Neil Sleat**
**Zeb Soanes**
**Diana Speed**
**Kathy Clugston**
**Susan Rae**
**Charles Carroll**

## EDITORS

**Jenny Abramsky** (1986–87)
**Phil Harding** (1987–93)
**Roger Mosey** (1993–97)
**John Barton** (1997–98)
**Rod Liddle** (1998–2002)
**Kevin Marsh** (2002–06)
**Ceri Thomas** (2006–12)
**Jamie Angus** (2012–17)
**Sarah Sands** (2017–)

# Premier League Football Clubs 2019/2020 Season

Arsenal

Aston Villa

AFC Bournemouth

Brighton and Hove
   Albion

Burnley

Chelsea

Crystal Palace

Everton

Leicester City

Liverpool

Manchester City

Manchester United

Newcastle United

Norwich City

Sheffield United

Southampton

Tottenham Hotspur

Watford

West Ham United

Wolverhampton
   Wanderers

# Women's Football World Cup Teams 2019

Argentina

Australia

Brazil

Cameroon

Canada

Chile

China PR

England

France

Germany

Italy

Jamaica

Japan

Korea Republic

Netherlands

New Zealand

Nigeria

Norway

Scotland

South Africa

Spain

Sweden

Thailand

USA

# The Solar System

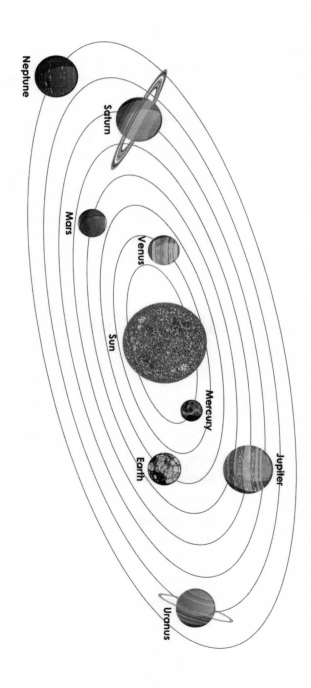

# World Map

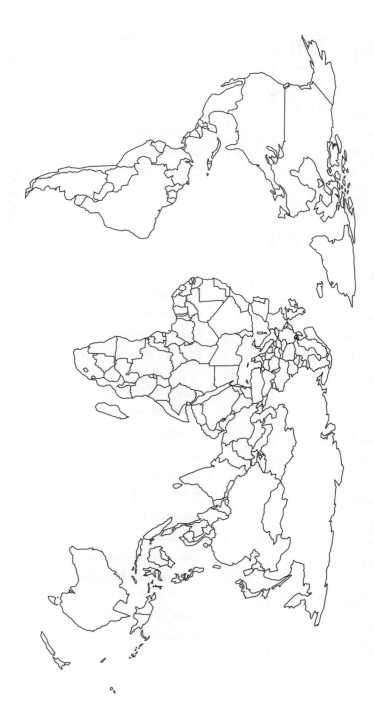

# Capital Cities

**Afghanistan** – Kabul

**Albania** – Tirana

**Algeria** – Algiers

**Andorra** – Andorra La Vella

**Angola** – Luanda

**Antigua and Barbuda** – St John's

**Argentina** – Buenos Aires

**Armenia** – Yerevan

**Australia** – Canberra

**Austria** – Vienna

**Azerbaijan** – Baku

**Bahamas, The** – Nassau

**Bahrain** – Manama

**Bangladesh** – Dhaka

**Barbados** – Bridgetown

**Belarus** – Minsk

**Belgium** – Brussels

**Belize** – Belmopan

**Benin** – Porto-Novo

**Bhutan** – Thimphu

**Bolivia** – La Paz/Sucre

**Bosnia-Herzegovina** – Sarajevo

**Botswana** – Gaborone

**Brazil** – Brasília

**Brunei** – Bandar Seri Begawan

**Bulgaria** – Sofia

**Burkina Faso** – Ouagadougou

**Burundi** – Bujumbura

**Cabo Verde** – Praia

**Cambodia** – Phnom Penh

**Cameroon** – Yaoundé

**Canada** – Ottawa

**Central African Republic** – Bangui

**Chad** – Ndjamena

**Chile** – Santiago

**China** – Beijing

**Colombia** – Bogotá

**Comoros** – Moroni

**Congo** – Brazzaville

**Congo, Democratic Republic of the** – Kinshasa

**Costa Rica** – San José

**Côte d'Ivoire** – Yamoussoukro

**Croatia** – Zagreb

**Cuba** – Havana

**Cyprus** – Nicosia

**Czechia** – Prague

**Denmark** – Copenhagen

**Djibouti** – Djibouti

**Dominica** – Roseau

**Dominican Republic** – Santo Domingo

**East Timor** – Dili

**Ecuador** – Quito

**Egypt** – Cairo

**El Salvador** – San Salvador

**Equatorial Guinea** – Malabo

**Eritrea** – Asmara

**Estonia** – Tallinn

**Eswatini (Swaziland)** – Mbabane

**Ethiopia** – Addis Ababa

**Fiji** – Suva

**Finland** – Helsinki

**France** – Paris

**Gabon** – Libreville

**Gambia, The** – Banjul

**Georgia** – Tbilisi

**Germany** – Berlin

**Ghana** – Accra

**Greece** – Athens

**Grenada** – St George's

**Guatemala** – Guatemala City

**Guinea** – Conakry

**Guinea-Bissau** – Bissau

**Guyana** – Georgetown

**Haiti** – Port-au-Prince

**Honduras** – Tegucigalpa

**Hungary** – Budapest

**Iceland** – Reykjavik

**India** – New Delhi

**Indonesia** – Jakarta

**Iran** – Tehran

**Iraq** – Baghdad

**Ireland** – Dublin

**Israel** – Jerusalem*

**Italy** – Rome

**Jamaica** – Kingston

**Japan** – Tokyo

**Jordan** – Amman

**Kazakhstan** – Astana

**Kenya** – Nairobi

**Kiribati** – Tarawa

**Korea, North** – Pyŏngyang

**Korea, South** – Seoul

**Kosovo** – Pristina

**Kuwait** – Kuwait City

**Kyrgyzstan** – Bishkek

**Laos** – Vientiane

**Latvia** – Riga

**Lebanon** – Beirut

**Lesotho** – Maseru

**Liberia** – Monrovia

**Libya** – Tripoli

**Liechtenstein** – Vaduz

**Lithuania** – Vilnius

**Luxembourg** – Luxembourg

**Macedonia, North** – Skopje

**Madagascar** – Antananarivo

* disputed

**Malawi** – Lilongwe

**Malaysia** – Kuala Lumpur/Putrajaya

**Maldives** – Malé

**Mali** – Bamako

**Malta** – Valletta

**Marshall Islands** – Majuro

**Mauritania** – Nouakchott

**Mauritius** – Port Louis

**Mexico** – Mexico City

**Micronesia** – Palikir

**Moldova** – Chisinau

**Monaco** – Monaco

**Mongolia** – Ulan Bator

**Montenegro** – Podgorica

**Morocco** – Rabat

**Mozambique** – Maputo

**Myanmar (Burma)** – Naypyidaw

**Namibia** – Windhoek

**Nauru** – Yaren

**Nepal** – Kathmandu

**Netherlands** – Amsterdam

**New Zealand** – Wellington

**Nicaragua** – Managua

**Niger** – Niamey

**Nigeria** – Abuja

**Norway** – Oslo

**Oman** – Muscat

**Pakistan** – Islamabad

**Palau** – Melekeok

**Panama** – Panamá

**Papua New Guinea** – Port Moresby

**Paraguay** – Asunción

**Peru** – Lima

**Philippines** – Manila

**Poland** – Warsaw

**Portugal** – Lisbon

**Qatar** – Doha

**Romania** – Bucharest

**Russia** – Moscow

**Rwanda** – Kigali

**St Kitts and Nevis** – Basseterre

**St Lucia** – Castries

**St Vincent and the Grenadines** – Kingstown

**Samoa** – Apia

**San Marino** – San Marino

**São Tomé and Príncipe** – São Tomé

**Saudi Arabia** – Riyadh

**Senegal** – Dakar

**Serbia** – Belgrade

**Seychelles** – Victoria

**Sierra Leone** – Freetown

**Singapore** – Singapore

**Slovakia** – Bratislava

**Slovenia** – Ljubljana

**Solomon Islands** – Honiara

**Somalia** – Mogadishu

**South Africa** – Cape Town/Pretoria/Bloemfontein

**Spain** – Madrid

**Sri Lanka** – Colombo

**Sudan** – Khartoum

**Sudan, South** – Juba

**Suriname** – Paramaribo

**Sweden** – Stockholm

**Switzerland** – Bern

**Syria** – Damascus

**Taiwan** – Taipei

**Tajikistan** – Dushanbe

**Tanzania** – Dodoma

**Thailand** – Bangkok

**Togo** – Lomé

**Tonga** – Nuku'alofa

**Trinidad and Tobago** – Port of Spain

**Tunisia** – Tunis

**Turkey** – Ankara

**Turkmenistan** – Ashgabat

**Tuvalu** – Fongafale

**Uganda** – Kampala

**Ukraine** – Kiev

**United Arab Emirates** – Abu Dhabi

**United Kingdom** – London

**United States of America** – Washington, DC

**Uruguay** – Montevideo

**Uzbekistan** – Tashkent

**Vanuatu** – Port-Vila

**Vatican City** – Vatican City

**Venezuela** – Caracas

**Vietnam** – Hanoi

**Yemen** – Sana'a

**Zambia** – Lusaka

**Zimbabwe** – Harare

# Useful Maths

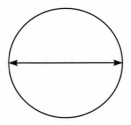

**Diameter**

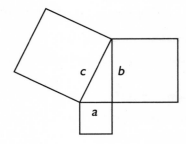

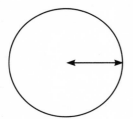

**Radius**

Pythagorus theorum for finding the area
of a right-angle triangle:
$$a^2 + b^2 = c^2$$

where each letter represents one side
of the triangle

distance = speed × time
$$\text{speed} = {}^{\text{distance}}\!/_{\text{time}}$$
$$\text{time} = {}^{\text{distance}}\!/_{\text{speed}}$$

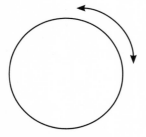

**Circumference**

Circumference =
π × diameter = 2π × radius

# Prime Numbers

A prime number is a whole number bigger than 1 that can be divided exactly by 1 and by itself but not by any other number.

| | | | | | |
|---|---|---|---|---|---|
| 2 | 59 | 137 | 227 | 313 | 419 |
| 3 | 61 | 139 | 229 | 317 | 421 |
| 5 | 67 | 149 | 233 | 331 | 431 |
| 7 | 71 | 151 | 239 | 337 | 433 |
| 11 | 73 | 157 | 241 | 347 | 439 |
| 13 | 79 | 163 | 251 | 349 | 443 |
| 17 | 83 | 167 | 257 | 353 | 449 |
| 19 | 89 | 173 | 263 | 359 | 457 |
| 23 | 97 | 179 | 269 | 367 | 461 |
| 29 | 101 | 181 | 271 | 373 | 463 |
| 31 | 103 | 191 | 277 | 379 | 467 |
| 37 | 107 | 193 | 281 | 383 | 479 |
| 41 | 109 | 197 | 283 | 389 | 487 |
| 43 | 113 | 199 | 293 | 397 | 491 |
| 47 | 127 | 211 | 307 | 401 | 499 |
| 53 | 131 | 223 | 311 | 409 | 503… |

NOTES

NOTES

# PUZZLE

# COMPILERS

## Professor Dave Abrahams

Professor David Abrahams is NM Rothschild & Sons Professor of Mathematical Sciences and Director of the Isaac Newton Institute, University of Cambridge, and a research visitor at the University of Manchester, where he has an active group working on the mathematical modelling of wave phenomena in industrial contexts. His work has wide-ranging application, from making domestic appliances quieter through to studying the melt rate of glaciers.

## Yin-Fung Au

Yin-Fung Au read Mathematics at Oxford University, and currently teaches the subject at a school in London.

## David Baynard

David Baynard is finishing a biotechnology PhD at Emmanuel College, Cambridge. In addition to puzzles, he constructs cryptic crosswords and cocktails, and helps maintain the Haskell software development tool, Stack. (www.baynard.dev)

## Sally Calder, Education Actuary, Institute and Faculty of Actuaries

Sally Calder graduated from Lady Margaret Hall, Oxford, with a Chemistry degree, and is a fellow of the Institute and Faculty of Actuaries. She currently works in actuarial professionalism and education and spent the earlier part of her career as a consultant in occupational pensions. She has always enjoyed brain-teasers and is passionate about making mathematics accessible and fun for all.

The IFoA is a leading international membership organization which educates, develops and regulates actuaries as experts in risk. This professional body aims to put the public interest first.

## Dr Elon Correa

Dr Elon Correa is Lecturer in Mathematics and Statistics, University of Salford.

## Dr Tom Crawford

Dr Tom Crawford is a Maths Tutor at the University of Oxford. His award-winning website tomrocksmaths.com features videos, podcasts, articles and puzzles designed to make maths more entertaining. Whether he's performing live as the Naked Mathematician with 'Equations Stripped', telling you fun facts about numbers, or getting another maths tattoo (6 and counting), it's safe to say Tom is always finding new ways to misbehave with numbers! Follow him on Facebook, Twitter, Instagram and YouTube @tomrocksmaths for the latest updates.

## Kyle D Evans

Kyle D Evans (@kyledevans) is an award-winning maths communicator and Head of Maths at Barton Peveril College www.kyledevans.com.

## Dr Geoff Evatt

Dr Geoff Evatt is an applied mathematician at the University of Manchester. His research focuses upon better understanding glaciers and ice sheet, and he leads the 'Lost Meteorites of Antarctica' project, an ambitious multidisciplinary study that hopes to discover meteorites trapped beneath the surface of Antarctica. Prior to Manchester, Geoff took his undergraduate and doctoral degrees at the University of Oxford, held a post-doctoral position at University College London, and worked in the City of London.

## David Feather

A mathematics education lecturer for some time at the University of the West of England, the University of Wales, Newport and the Open University, David is now retired.

## Dr Shaun Fitzgerald

Director of the Royal Institution and a Fellow of the Royal Academy of Engineering, Dr Shaun Fitzgerald is also a Royal Academy of Engineering Visiting Professor in Sustainable Buildings at Cambridge University and a Fellow of Girton College. Prior to joining the Royal Institution he founded and led Breathing Buildings, a hybrid ventilation company which pioneered new technology for buildings. As CEO he assisted the government in the review of regulations for school buildings in order to ensure provision of well-ventilated and low-energy teaching environments.

### Dr Nicos Georgiou

Dr Nicos Georgiou is a Senior Lecturer in Mathematics at the University of Sussex. Nicos's research is on Probability Theory, an area he was drawn into by its many counterintuitive examples, particularly in the area of random games and gambling strategies. Nicos is an avid puzzle-solver, and he particularly enjoys puzzles, magic tricks and murder mysteries that can be elegantly explained and generalised with a hidden mathematical theorem or just pure, cold logic.

### Dr Russell Gerrard

Russell Gerrard was a Wrangler at the University of Cambridge and remained at the same institution to complete a PhD in Stochastic Processes. After a year at the University of Sussex he spent nine months at Moscow State University, followed by six months at the University of Zurich. He subsequently joined City, University of London in the Department of Mathematics and currently works in the Faculty of Actuarial Science and Insurance of Cass Business School, which forms part of City. His research focuses on applications of probability and statistics, primarily to problems of an actuarial nature. He has performed as a Principal Examiner for the Institute and Faculty of Actuaries and has served as Associate Dean for the undergraduate programme at Cass.

### Mr Ryan Glass

Originally from Ballyclare, Northern Ireland, Ryan Glass studied Mathematics at Queen's University Belfast, completing a masters degree with first class honours. He completed his PGCE at the same university, before moving to England to begin his teaching career. His first teaching job was at Haileybury College, before moving to Sevenoaks School in 2016, where he is currently Second in Department. Maths has always been a passion and teaching has always been a dream career. He says: 'Sevenoaks School is a great institution to be associated with, and alongside the birth of my beautiful daughter, Phoebe, in January 2018, and with all the constant support of all my friends and family over the years, I am certainly very blessed!'

### Daniel Griller

Daniel Griller is an educator, problem-composer and author of the bestselling puzzle book *Elastic Numbers and Problem Solving in GCSE Mathematics*. Having read mathematics at Trinity College, Cambridge, he now teaches the subject at a school in the UK. He has coached teams to successive national titles at the FSMP/UKMT Senior Team Maths Challenge and a Hans Woyda Maths Competition crown. An experienced problem-designer, his inventions have appeared in the British Maths Olympiad, the Senior Maths Challenge and the *Guardian*.

### David Hargreaves

David is a mathematician who graduated from Cambridge University in 1991 before embarking on careers in the police, teaching and the actuarial profession. He returned to teaching in 2013, becoming a visiting lecturer at Cass Business School, where he has taught across a wide range of actuarial subjects. Outside of work, David has developed a computer program to play poker (which is the only piece of mathematics he has done to interest non-mathematicians) and is trying to eliminate the housing crisis by getting politicians to understand the interaction of housing benefit and fractional reserve banking (currently with no success).

### Dr Steve Humble MBE

A senior lecturer and Head of Education at Newcastle University, Dr Steve Humble carries out research in sub-Saharan Africa, South America and India concerning parental choice and schooling. He teaches undergraduate and postgraduate courses in advanced quantitative methods, and has worked with the British government to investigate, support and develop educational improvements.

His first book, *The Experimenter's A-Z of Mathematics: Maths Activities with Computer Support*, was published in 2002. He is a fellow of The Institute of Mathematics and its Applications (IMA) and for eight years he wrote fortnightly newspaper columns for eight years as @DrMaths and drmaths.org. His latest book, *Quantitative Analysis of Questionnaires* (2020), explains how to use statistical techniques to explore structures and relationships in surveys, and is published by Routledge.

### Hugh Hunt

Hugh Hunt is Reader in Engineering Dynamics and Vibration at Trinity College, Cambridge.

### Prathan Jarupoonphol

Prathan Jarupoonphol is a Ph.D. candidate in mathematics at the University of Sheffield.

### Robin Michaelson

Robin Michaelson graduated from Corpus Christi College, Oxford, and is a Fellow of the Institute of Actuaries, having spent his working career in life insurance and reinsurance, in both the UK and Australia. In retirement, he is a Visiting Lecturer on Actuarial Practicality at the Cass Business School, in the Faculty of Actuarial Science and Insurance. He has always been interested in mathematical puzzles and teasers, and in how they can relate to everyday life.

### Susan Okereke

Susan Okereke has taught maths for over 12 years, with students ranging from primary and secondary pupils to NEET (not in employment, education or training), young people and pensioners. Through her teaching, writing and presenting Susan aims to help people understand that maths is an interesting and powerful subject, relevant to people's everyday lives. This mission led her to co-host the Maths Appeal podcast with fellow puzzle maker Bobby Seagull. Susan recently completed a Master's degree in Teaching at the UCL Institute of Education and has collaborated with organisations such as the British Museum and the Museum of London to design contextual maths resources based on exhibitions. This year Susan contributed to the book *A Practical Guide to Teaching Secondary Mathematics* by writing the chapter on 'Pupil Led ICT'.

### The Maths Department, Oxford High School GDST

Maths is the most popular A Level subject at Oxford High School, the leading girls' independent school in Oxford. The Maths Department came up with the puzzles collectively and have enjoyed sharing them with the girls. @ohsmaths.

### Bobby Seagull

Bobby Seagull is a school maths teacher and doctorate student in Mathematics Education at Cambridge University. He is an ambassador for the charities National Numeracy, Potential Plus UK, Sponsorstars and a UK Libraries Champion (CILIP).

He is also an ambassador for Shell Bright Ideas Challenge and Explore Learning National Young Mathematicians' Award. He is a trustee of the charity UpRising, a governor of Newham College and the co-founder of the social enterprise OxFizz.

Bobby presents an Open University personal finance course for young adults and is a Financial Times Money columnist. He occasionally reviews newspapers on BBC Breakfast and has on appeared on Celebrity University Challenge for Comic Relief.

He is co-author of *The Monkman & Seagull Quiz Book* and co-presenter of the BBC TV series *Monkman & Seagull's Genius Guide to Britain* and the second series, *Genius Guide to the Age of Invention*. His own book *The Life-Changing Magic Of Numbers* is an Amazon bestseller. He co-hosts the Maths Appeal podcast. Outside of all these things numerical, he is a long-suffering West Ham fan.

Follow his adventures via Twitter & Instagram on @bobby_seagull, LinkedIn page, YouTube channel and website www.bobbyseagull.com.

## Dr Andrew Smedley

Dr Andrew Smedley is currently a Research Associate at the School of Mathematics, University of Manchester, working on the 'Lost Meteorites of Antarctica' project. He completed his undergraduate degree in Natural Science at the University of Cambridge before studying for his PhD as an atmospheric scientist. His research centres on the interaction between sunlight, clouds in the atmosphere and, most recently, ice in the cryosphere.

## School of Mathematics and Statistics at the University of Sheffield

The puzzles that appear have come from contributors ranging form undergraduates to emeritus professors via every academic rank and technical staff position in between. They were developed at weekly coffee mornings, with further contributions and improvements suggested from a broad range of people.

## Dr Lynda White

Dr Lynda White is principal Teaching Fellow in Experimental Design in the Department of Mathematics at Imperial College London.

**BBC RADIO 4**

An Hachette UK Company
www.hachette.co.uk

First published in Great Britain in 2019 by Cassell,
an imprint of Octopus Publishing Group Ltd
Carmelite House
50 Victoria Embankment
London EC4Y 0DZ
www.octopusbooks.co.uk

Chapter introductions by Tom Feilden

ISBN 978-1-78840-065-7

A CIP catalogue record for this book is available from the
British Library

Printed and bound in the United Kingdom

10 9 8 7 6 5 4 3 2 1

**Senior Commissioning Editor** Romilly Morgan
**Editor** Ella Parsons
**Designer** Jack Storey
**Typesetter** Jeremy Tilston
**Copy Editor** Sonya Newland
**Production Controller** Serena Savini

## Picture Credits